The Meaning
of Trump

The Meaning of Trump

Brian Francis Culkin

Winchester, UK
Washington, USA

First published by Zero Books, 2018
Zero Books is an imprint of John Hunt Publishing Ltd., No. 3 East St., Alresford,
Hampshire SO24 9EE, UK
office1@jhpbooks.net
www.johnhuntpublishing.com
www.zero-books.net

For distributor details and how to order please visit the 'Ordering' section on our website.

Text copyright: Brian Francis Culkin 2017

ISBN: 978 1 78904 046 3
978 1 78904 047 0 (ebook)
Library of Congress Control Number: 2018933757

A CIP catalogue record for this book is available from the British Library.

Design: Stuart Davies

Printed and bound by CPI Group (UK) Ltd, Croydon, CR0 4YY, UK

We operate a distinctive and ethical publishing philosophy in
all areas of our business, from our global network of authors to
production and worldwide distribution.

Contents

Introduction

In the past century, we thought democracy and socialism had defeated nationalism. Wrong.[1]
Franco "Bifo" Berardi

In Kevin Kelly's recent book *The Inevitable* he presents a forecast of 12 trends that will emerge in the coming decades from the continued expansion of digital technologies and globalized capitalism.[2] Although Kelly is often unabashedly optimistic when commenting upon the potential socioeconomic and cultural effects this ongoing information revolution will have, he nevertheless acknowledges a certain existential crisis that this very same transformation is now producing, and will further produce. It is an impending, irreducible crisis that essentially divides humanity into two overlapping and competing factions; two factions that Kelly terms The People of the Book and The People of the Screen.

The People of the Book, for Kelly, are simply those individuals, organizations, and ideologies that still maintain a fidelity to the various forms of culture and economic production that were inherent to humanity prior to the widespread arrival of digital technologies: a reverence for printed books, newspapers, and periodicals; an allegiance to the rule of law as well as to classic interpretations of ethics and morality; and a desire to engage in an economic system that is local in its operation and "analog" in its underlying logic – such as a small farm or a productive factory.

On the contrary, The People of the Screen are those who have rather adopted the ideologies and practices that have emerged over the past decades in response to both the proliferation of networked technologies into our social and cultural spaces as well as widespread economic globalization. The People of the

Screen prefer to perform their labor while connected into a global network; they gravitate toward digital content in lieu of the written word; they tend to reject traditional norms and values in favor of a pervasive social fluidity; and they are often urban based and individually centered versus having historical ties to a local community or an allegiance to a defined family network:

> But today most of us have become People of the Screen. People of the Screen tend to ignore the classic logic of books or the reverence of copies; they prefer the dynamic flux of pixels. They gravitate toward movie screens, TV screens, computer screens, iPhone screens, VR goggle screens, tablet screens, and in the near future massive Day-Glo megapixel screens plastered on every surface. Screen culture is a world of constant flux, of endless sound bites, quick cuts, and half-baked ideas. It is a flow of tweets, headlines, Instagrams, casual texts, and floating first impressions. Notions don't stand alone but are massively interlinked to everything else; truth is not delivered by authors and authorities but is assembled in real time piece by piece by the audience themselves. People of the Screen make their own content and construct their own truth. Fixed copies don't matter as much as flowing screens. Screen culture is fast, like a 30 second movie trailer, and as liquid and open ended as a Wikipedia page.[3]

One cannot help but notice a profound contradiction when we apply Kelly's dichotomy of contemporary subjectivity onto the cultural symbolism of Donald Trump. That is to say, by all accounts, Donald Trump is the very definition of a "Person of the Screen": a Reality Television star who lives out much of his social existence as a public spectacle and media sound bite; an individual who communicates his most intimate and personal ideas through his social media feed; and a person who happily allows his own image to be endlessly circulated through the machinery of the global media apparatus.

Yet, and strangely enough, Donald Trump's rhetoric and the core of his political platform was in many respects addressed to what now comprises the disintegrating population of The People of the Book: the everyday, working-class Americans who were ultimately drawn to his message for the very reason that they have been progressively left behind by the economics and technology that defines contemporary screen culture. This is not to say, by any stretch of the imagination, that Trump supporters were actually conscious of this disjuncture; that they abstained from participating in the emergent screen society and instead read Dickens by night and the daily newspaper by morning over a cup of coffee at the family breakfast table.

But that is the whole point.

In other words, both Trump and his supporters, for the most part, *did not even know what their problem was or what it was they even wanted.* All they could ultimately articulate was a pervasive feeling of frustration and resentment — often encapsulated in one-line slogans such as "Draining the Swamp" — that was to be effectively channeled at the state of contemporary identity politics, contemporary media practices, and the contemporary economic system that has ravaged their small communities and towns over the past several decades. Their recourse was thus to gravitate toward a political message that promised them a return of collective national identity, a return of law and order, and a return to an industrial-based economic system that was once the base of their collective livelihood.[4] In short, what they were promised was *a return to the past;* a past that once existed in their minds prior to the rise of digital technologies and neoliberal globalization. One can only marvel at the fact that this very political and spiritual message — that of a collective return to a set of traditional socioeconomic practices and national purity — was delivered by a Tweeting, Reality Television star.

Liberal critics have categorically and consistently dismissed the resurgence of populist discourse in American politics that Trump's rise signifies — a trajectory that can be gauged in recent years from the evolution of neoconservatism, to the Tea Party movement, to Trump's brand of nationalism — as a dangerous and reactive stance against both cultural and economic progress. They have made the claim that this type of retroactive rhetoric and politics has no place in a fast globalizing world where multiculturalism, social and cultural fluidity, and market dynamics have become the grounding principals of the new global order. But what if the very opposite was true? That is to say, what if this resurgence of American populism that is apparently so disdained by liberal commentators was actually part of the very same process that these same liberal commentators unilaterally defend?

> ...the problem is rather to conceive of this populism as a new form of "false transparency," which, far from presenting a serious obstacle to (liberal) capitalist modernization, paves the way for it.[5]

In other words, the recent surge of American nationalism and its accompanying populist rhetoric runs directly *with* the progressive dynamism of (liberal) global capitalism. So, what is thus essential when reading the cultural symbolism of Donald Trump and his unique brand of virtualized populist-fundamentalism is *not* to see his political ascendancy as some external intrusion into the normal order of things; but rather to see his dramatic political entrance as simply a part of a singular ongoing sociopolitical process: to perceive that his emergence onto the national political stage was *synonymous* with the general trajectory of our societal, economic, and technological development that has been part and parcel of neoliberal globalization over the past four decades.

Writing about Donald Trump brings about a rather peculiar

4

feeling in myself, and that peculiarity has to do with the asymmetry of how seriously I take the task. In a certain respect, writing about the politics of Trump — his unhinged personality, or the childlike rhetoric that he often uses to communicate important matters of foreign and domestic policy — it is nearly impossible to keep up even the appearance of a serious commentary. It can't help but become equal parts absurdity and comedy when encountering the concrete fact that this man is now the leader of the free world. Yet, and in exact opposition to the absurdity of the situation, writing about and attempting to make sense of the cultural symbolism that Donald Trump represents in the early decades of the twenty-first century is a deadly serious matter. And it is a deadly serious matter precisely because humanity, in this very moment, is fast approaching a crisis point. It is a multifaceted crisis that is equally ecological, economic, political, psychological, and technological. But ultimately, the planetary crisis that is now revealing itself in no uncertain terms in various instances and guises across the globe — while being ruthlessly suppressed at the very same time — is ultimately a crisis that can only be appropriately named as an existential breaking point; what we could even term as an *ontological crisis*. It is a crisis of our collective *Being.* And the underlying nature of this crisis can be most effectively characterized as the very same transformation referenced by Kevin Kelly: that The People of the Book are now being displaced wholesale by The People of the Screen.[6] But when trying to conceptualize this emerging division of humanity it would be a critical mistake to assume that this looming division of planetary society is an external one; that there is a clear demarcation point or a precise catalog of distinguishing features that now separates The People of the Book from The People of the Screen. More appropriately, this is a division that is now being inscribed *within* us all: we are now, each and every one of us, caught between two worlds that are rapidly diverging from one another while tearing us apart — our psychological health, social fabric, and economic productivity — in the process. In other words, we are now painfully discovering that there is no possibility of a happy medium between *The New York Times* and our Facebook feeds; there is no real common ground to be found between fully automative factories and a stable American middle class; and there is no real symmetry between an engaged politics and civic responsibility with widespread digital consumerism and celebrity culture. And this emerging recognition, a recognition that is simultaneously repressed and displaced at every turn, is also producing a fracture not only in our political, economic, and social structures — but also within our minds and hearts.

This ongoing and truly radical reconstitution of human productivity, consciousness, and culture is what has emerged in response to global capitalism's transformation over the past several decades; as it has moved beyond its industrial phase and into its postindustrial, technological phase in the present. The core of this transformation has been essentially two-fold. The first part is that the entire range of human experience has been progressively reduced to pure economic efficiency; the manifold of human life has been reconditioned to only exist within an economic framework and a consciousness that principally reflects the state of global markets and capitalist logic. The now infamous line from Chicago-born hip hop artist Kanye West perfectly summarizes this point — "I'm not a businessman, *I'm a business, man*":[7] our very lives and bodies have become "businesses" unto themselves in the era of twenty-first century global capitalism. In other words, the practices and logic of the economy are no longer confined to what occurs during a 9–5 shift. Such logic has now extended beyond the perimeter of the office building or the factory, the very places where it was once confined in the previous order of capitalism, and now lives and breathes as the all-encompassing fact of our lives. From the constant and pervasive exposure to this logic we have all become, unwillingly and unknowingly, *homo economus*: humans who now regard their own lives — and the lives of others — as purely instrumental, as "subjects of neoliberal achievement" whose primary purpose in life is to produce, compete, and create within the parameters of a purely capitalist logic.

The second part of this same transformation is how digital technology now determines and mediates this very same reduction of human life into a purely economic framework: the constant generation of quantifiable sets of data, discrete personal information that can be aggregated and monetized by third-party corporations and tech companies, while at the very same time creating the very infrastructure within which the majority of our socioeconomic interaction now occurs: within the virtual realm, in our social media feeds, and on the various global networks. That is to say, the recent metamorphosis of human life into primarily existing as an extension of game theory, within a purely economic schema, would have been *impossible* without the accompanying technological transformation: digital and networked technologies are the material forces that have provided the framework for this transformation to so effortlessly emerge in recent decades.

In a certain respect, the election of Donald Trump can be seen as symbolic of this very same uncomfortable and traumatic passage that has occurred in the early decades of the twenty-first century; a passage in which humanity itself is being drawn further and further into the horizon of neoliberal globalization and Silicon Valley logic.

As we collectively leave behind the world of books and the rule of law for a world of pixilated screens and computational technology, a sense of collective panic sets in, confusion reigns supreme, and a whole range of psychological pathologies suddenly and dramatically infect global culture as we attempt to make sense of (or simply block out) this ongoing transformation. As new markets and new technologies emerge ever more rapidly, we are conditioned by economic and political authority to adjust, evolve, and adapt — *or else.*

And it is *only* in this environment of collective fear — socially decomposing, spiritually and ecologically fragmented, psychically overwhelmed by the trove of the most banal data and content that we are daily exposed to — that a person like Donald Trump could be elected President.[8] And a person such as Trump could become President not simply because of the fact that he radically simplifies and dumbs down these complex socioeconomic changes for his supporters to effectively grasp, but also because of the fact that he openly *disrespects* them: he locates the incongruities and aberrations of neoliberalism and exposes them in the most brutal (and occasionally comical) of ways.

What is ironic here is only the fact that Trump *appears* to be a reactionary force, a force that is opposed to the core features of this very same development. But this reactionary gesture that Donald Trump is said to embody is fundamentally misleading. It is misleading because, despite his rhetoric, Trump absolutely signifies the universal frame that is now emerging within the new global order at its most elementary level. That is to say, for instance, there can be no doubt that Trump's attitude toward women and minorities is fundamentally reactionary, a giant leap backwards in public civility and in the struggle for equality. But yet, in his work as a global real estate developer and as a representation of contemporary media practices, Donald Trump is practically of the *avant garde:* in this regard Donald Trump actually signifies the most *progressive* elements of twenty-first century global capitalism and culture, a fact that is often conveniently overlooked when analyzing his political rise.

From this perspective, one can only find it extremely curious how Donald Trump and so many contemporary Republicans have the audacity to actually see themselves as "conservatives." In one sense they claim they want to maintain, even enforce if they had the chance, a set of traditional moral principals and normative behaviors that would serve to appropriately moderate civil society. Yet, in another sense, the exotic financial products they unleash daily from Wall Street and the multinational corporations they defend are what are primarily responsible for the very same moral blackout they endlessly complain about. The fact of the matter is that people like Donald Trump are the most impassioned and committed revolutionaries; they are the true radicals of twenty-first century globalized capitalism.

This is the true paradox of the situation at hand: the de-politicized economic logic and style of media engagement that Trump signifies in his very person — what we can effectively describe as being homologous to the core ideology of neoliberal globalization — is exactly what comes to greatly intensify and even radicalize those very same reactionary outbursts that Trump has engaged in throughout his campaign and first year as President. In the now standard critiques of Donald Trump that permeate the liberal mediascape of contemporary American society, one cannot help but feel that these critiques are missing the entirety of the forest as they endlessly point out the broken trees.

I will conclude this introduction with a rather bold and provocative statement: that Donald Trump may in fact signify something more disarming, and far more horrifying, than anything we have given him credit for thus far. I will even make the incredible claim that Donald Trump may in fact symbolize the emerging fissure of humanity with itself and its past. That is to say, what the election of Donald Trump may actually mean is that the *condition of humanity* is now undergoing a metamorphosis unlike any other in our history. We are in the process — through the combinatory forces of a global capitalism fully linked in with the power of computational technologies – of becoming something Other: human beings whose lives and brains are now plugged into a sprawling global network and are now suffering, and will further suffer, the consequences of such a radical transformation.

What this Other-ness will ultimately entail is not fully answered as of yet; we can only see glimpses that are both horrifying and potentially even promising. But what we can now see for certain is that the early decades of the twenty-first century are the very period in which the struggle to define what is to come for humanity will be determined.

Of course, we know how dangerous Donald Trump and his policies could potentially be. But what we also must realize is that Donald Trump is a *sign* — a public figure who nearly registers in the field of ancient mythology versus contemporary global politics — whereby we can encounter the limits of our cultural pathologies, the reality of our social and economic inequalities, and the tragic fact of our collective spiritual decomposition.

For what reason has this collective encounter with Donald Trump taken place? This is the precise question that remains unanswered as of yet. The future — a global destination that now appears increasingly dangerous and hopeless, not to mention completely unimaginable from our present vantage point — is fundamentally a space of potentiality, a space that has yet to be fully inscribed.[9] Could it be that Donald Trump is only symbolic of a chance to re-write the history of this very future, that his political rise represents a chance for humanity to re-ask questions that we have been told were already answered?

These are the very questions that must be brought to the surface if we are to excavate the true meaning of Donald Trump.

The meaning of Trump

Who is Donald Trump? Or, perhaps more appropriately, the question should be *what* is Donald Trump? That is to say, what does his emergence as an American political phenomenon signify on the symbolic level?

There is not a straightforward answer. How could the alliance between a Manhattan billionaire, a twenty-first century Reality Television star, and a fragmented assemblage of displaced workers throughout the American Rust Belt be straightforward? Yet, nevertheless, this is precisely what happened — one of the many asymmetrical pieces that came to form the 2016 election puzzle — so to deliver the forty-fifth Presidency to Donald Trump.

One cannot help but scratch one's head at such an absurd situation. In many respects Donald Trump is representative of the very forces — the exponential breakdown of local culture and local sensibility by the global media apparatus; the continuous expansion of global capitalism in the forms of outsourcing, privatization, and deregulation; the ongoing consolidation of political and economic power into the hands of a supranational global oligarchy[10] — that have directly led to the socioeconomic displacement of the very same American workers that he mobilized into his core political base; not to mention exacerbating the pervasive sense of cultural impotence that has attracted a new generation of white nationalists into our political discourse.[11]

In other words, Donald Trump, and strangely enough, has helped to create the very conditions for his populist inspired socioeconomic and political critiques to be taken seriously: *he is a perfect representation of what his politics is said to struggle against.*

Throughout his writing contemporary philosopher Slavoj Zizek has made use of the Gospel line "for they know not what they do,"[12] as a way to explain how ideology functions. Ideology is usually regarded in most political commentary as an adherence to a set of clearly discernible beliefs or sociopolitical axioms, as in having an ideological fidelity to Nazism or Soviet communism. But for Zizek, one also follows ideology when they do not even realize it: ideology is a collective pattern of thinking and doing that has become so part and parcel to everyday experience that it fades into the background and thus appears as the naturalized frame of one's experience. Meaning, the most powerful ideology occurs when we are not even conscious of believing in it or acting it out in our lives.

With that there was something profoundly ideological following Trump's victory when his two sons — Donald Jr. and Eric, now the principals of the Trump business empire — announced that they were planning on opening a chain of hotels in what many have now referred to as "Trump-land." Or, what was once simply known as middle America:

> Trump Hotels, the brand run by President Donald Trump's two sons, has announced that it will start a new mid-scale brand.
>
> The chain will be called American IDEA, and will debut with three properties in the Mississippi Delta area - in Cleveland, Clarksdale and Greenville. The company says it has already signed the agreements, and that the concept will be "rooted in local history and neighborly service"...
>
> "We look forward to leveraging our expertise and experience across the various segments of the hotel business and bringing our trademark hospitality to many more guests, owners and markets across the nation," says Trump Hotels CEO Eric Danziger.
>
> The announcement was made during the 39th Annual NYU International Hospitality Industry Investment Conference, a time when many real estate deals are hatched.[13]

What we see in the above passage is more complex than what

may appear upon first glance: not simply that of a shameless and opportunistic power grab by the two Trump sons; a direct leveraging of their father's Presidential victory into the demographic area most associated with his core political base. What we also see in the above passage is the very same ideological mechanism that drove displaced blue-collar voters toward Trump in the first place.

Although Trump was sometimes correct in pointing out throughout his campaign the profound injustice that workers and small farmers have experienced throughout much of America from the cumulative effects of neoliberal globalization[14] — the closing and outsourcing of American productive factories to the Third World for the purpose of reducing labor costs and evading regulations, the ongoing disintegration of the American middle and working class, the rhetorical hypocrisy and economic collusion of Wall Street, Silicon Valley, and the mainstream media to the detriment of ordinary Americans — what he was not able to articulate in any coherent way was the other side of the very same neoliberal coin: like the multinational corporations like Walmart that have moved in and radically transformed the communal fabric of thousands of small towns throughout America to their own detriment.[15] In other words, in Trump's very remedial view of cause and effect, the continual outsourcing of American jobs throughout these regions as the result of free trade deals and globalization is unacceptable; a direct affront to the stability and dignity of the American worker. Yet when these same socioeconomic forces come to small town America heralding the promise of "jobs"[16] in the form of a Walmart, in the innumerable national chain retail stores or restaurants you now see on the side of any American highway or strip mall, or as in the new brand of hotels now in development by the Trump Corporation, it is rather seen as "investment in America" and a beneficial development.

But this is the type of disconnected logic and ideological blindness that now defines contemporary American politics, a collective blindness that always produces the very same question for each major party to grapple with: how do we mitigate, through ideology and partisan political rhetoric, the most problematic features of twenty-first century global capitalism; how do we gloss over the profound inconsistencies and antagonisms that now define the functioning of the global economy in order to produce a coherent world view for our frustrated political base?

In many ways we seem to be at a dead end here. There are no clear political solutions as to how we move forward in the present era of a global capitalism that has now become fully synchronistic with the power, algorithmic intelligence, and sheer speed of networked technologies. From the result of this novel dynamic, social and political life has all but lost contact with its public dimension. Now thoroughly privatized within the coordinates of a corporate logic, the production of our shared knowledge, our culture, and even our most personal and most intimate relationships are in the process of being lost to the demands of shareholder value, technological efficiency, and bottom lines. We are now hyper-connected, but as a result we have lost our autonomy and our ability to be emphatic; to listen to each other's struggles and respond with dignity, clarity, and vision.[17]

In this very context, what Trump may in fact bear witness to is an emergent political paradox: the seeming impossibility of bringing forth a new kind of politics in the present moment that can effectively respond to the growing friction that is now revealing itself in no uncertain terms across the planet: continued neoliberal globalization or Donald Trump's brand of nationalist-populism.[18]

The election of Donald Trump does not only demonstrate the fact of a profound crisis that directly mirrors the overall state of American political life (or even the fact of the long-gestating crisis regarding the core principals of neoliberal globalization that have exploded to the surface with his bombastic and ungrounded critiques). What the election of Donald Trump may truly signify is a *crisis of humanity*, an unfolding and exponentially intensifying crisis of our shared future together on Planet Earth, and with that, the importance of thinking a new kind of politics that can emerge into both theory and practice.

I have divided what follows into three parts:

1. The transformation of global capitalism. The ongoing mutation of global capitalism that has been occurring throughout Western economies since the 1980s is what we could characterize as being a shift from industrial capitalism to postindustrial capitalism; from Fordism to post-Fordism; from a national economy defined by productive technologies rooted in time and place (as in the factory or office building located in a particular town) to the emergence of a global economy defined by the proliferation of digital technologies,[19] the ascendancy of unregulated and internationalized financial markets, and de-centered media content produced and accessed by individualized cognitive professionals.[20] Among the numerous deleterious effects this transformation has brought forth, perhaps the most harrowing is how our public spaces and personal relationships have become increasingly mediated by the combined forces of digital surveillance and a corporate logic: mass privatization is now the unquestioned norm across the majority of our public and personal spaces. Under these conditions our social life — as in our interpersonal relationships, our local cultures, and most certainly our collective psychological health — becomes exponentially deprived of its autonomy, vitality, and even sanity.[21] We have been forced to progressively migrate our experiences to the virtual sphere (as in the social medias for example) while abandoning the flesh of our bodies and the reality of our surroundings: our capacity for empathy

and sensitivity becomes exponentially foreclosed within these socioeconomic conditions. And, perhaps emblematic of this mass migration of humanity to the virtual realm is the phenomenon of Reality Television and the symbolism of none other than Donald Trump.

2. The discourses of Donald Trump. It is interesting to take note of how Donald Trump, in his very person, in many ways signifies the very *opposite* of his political project. That is to say, how can the politics of a billionaire real estate developer and global media personality be symmetrical with the politics of displaced American workers, farmers, and the ever growing middle-class casualties of neoliberalism?[22] In a simplistic way, Donald Trump's political project directly appealed to the making of a nostalgic return to the days when hard-working men labored in set 9-5 shifts, when nuclear families sat down for a shared meal every Sunday evening, and when Old Glory flew proudly outside of every white picket fence. For the contemporary American citizen to whom this nostalgic appeal was directly addressed — the countless middle- and working-class Americans who desperately wanted to enact that very same return that Donald Trump spoke to — there was, in their worldview, a singular cultural figure standing in the way: the coastal liberal elite. Or, to put it another way: Manhattan billionaires like Donald Trump. In other words, the politics articulated by Donald Trump — a vague populism with little intellectual foundation or historical context — has very little in common with either his personal biography or history as an American business mogul.

3. The resistance to Trump. What we should uncomfortably recognize about much of the widespread resistance to the

Trump presidency is how it's not an authentic resistance in the deepest sense of the word. On the contrary, what we can see in both the standard liberal-democratic resistance and the faux outrage of the American conservative[23] to Donald Trump's crude politics is rather that of a desperate attempt to *re-establish the status quo*. The re-establishment of the "status quo" being, essentially, a smooth return to the basic frame of neoliberal globalization whereby the trifecta of power between Silicon Valley, Wall Street, and the global media can continue to operate smoothly in the absence of any disturbance from a populist inspired politician like Donald Trump. But what we often fail to see is that these are the very same conditions that helped fuel the rise of Donald Trump, that these are the very same forces that opened the possibility whereby his politics could even be heard. This is not to say I don't think we should resist the politics of Trump; we must, or else it seems that the future of our planet could be put in imminent danger. The question I will pose to conclude this book is *what kind* of resistance will it be? Will it be a resistance that opens up new ways to think about global society, the state of our interconnected humanity, and what novel ideas could potentially disclose a new kind of political vision for America and the world? Or, will it be a reactionary, pseudo-progressive resistance that simply seeks to reestablish the old status quo, the very same status quo that helped to give rise to the politics of Trump in the first place?

In many ways the entrance of Donald Trump onto the national political stage signifies a kind of culmination, and perhaps even a breaking point, to the proliferation of neoliberalism — the mass privatization, deregulation, outsourcing, and simulation — that has infected both American and planetary society since the 1980s. We, as both Americans and representations of humanity itself, have become psychologically and spiritually fragmented, torn apart by difference, and haunted by the spectral presence of information overload in the age of digital capitalism. Amidst this profound sociopolitical confusion, this interpersonal disconnection, and this regression to misogynist and racist outbursts, the figure of Donald Trump emerges as a symbolic figure bearing witness to the extent of our social fragmentation, personal loneliness, and cultural alienation:

> This is why the social body has lost contact with its brain: the production of knowledge and technology is deployed in a privatized corporate space which is disconnected from the needs of society, and responds only to economic requirements of profit maximization. Disconnected from the body, the social brain becomes incapable of autonomy. Disconnected from the brain, the social body becomes incapable of strategy or empathy…The hyper-stimulated body is simultaneously alone and hyper-connected: the more it is connected, the more it is alone.[24]

I think one of the things we must clearly recognize at this stage is that there is no "going back to normal" after the electoral victory of Donald Trump; there is simply no possibility of returning to a national political climate in which the residue of his presence and rhetoric will not be felt. Like a life altering trauma experienced by the individual, the national life and political climate we once knew as Americans will never be the same again: it is only a collective and political healing that will suffice to remedy the profound damage that has been done. And in direct relation to this traumatic political intrusion there is simply no way to explain away this trauma — to displace the cause of Donald Trump's rise to political power onto Trump himself, or by characterizing his supporters with categorical and inflammatory terms — without fully taking into account the socioeconomic, technological, and political factors that opened up the possibility for his politics to even be taken seriously: Donald Trump's rise is directly symmetrical to the catastrophic failure of *both* major political parties to effectively respond to the growing complications produced by global capitalism, global technology, and global militarism over the past several decades. Voters gravitated to his style of "just telling it how it is" rhetoric as a referendum against the cold and formal discourses of technocratic specialization and politically correct language, a set of discourses that have fundamentally failed to produce a coherent political vision for American voters in the twenty-first century.

There is no real substantial positive content in the politics of Donald Trump; his ideology and political project does not signify anything new; they do not signify anything that attempts to bring forth any real legislative novelty. His entire politics can be regarded as an attempt to *negate* the cancerous growth of twenty-first century neoliberalism; and therefore, paradoxically, as an attempt to *negate his very self.*

1

The transformation of global capitalism

The revolution that began with machines and chemicals proposes now to continue with automation, computers, and biotechnology. That this has been and is a revolution is undeniable. It has not been merely a "scientific revolution" as its proponents like to call it, but also an economic one, involving great and profound changes in property ownership and the distribution of wealth.[25]
Wendell Berry, What Are People For?

What excites us is some sort of technological revolution: the fossil fuel revolution, the automotive revolution, the assembly line revolution, the antibiotic revolution, the sexual revolution, the computer revolution...the genomic revolution, and so on. But these revolutions – all with something to sell that people or their government "must" buy – are mere episodes of the one truly revolutionary revolution in the history of the human race: the Industrial Revolution, which has proceeded from the beginning with only two purposes: to replace human workers with machines, and to market its products, regardless of their usefulness or their effects, at the highest possible profit – and so to concentrate wealth into even fewer hands.[26]
Wendell Berry, Our Only World

The election of Ronald Reagan in 1980 can now be perceived as a watershed moment — a political event that signified a passage from one order of things to the next — in which we can now see the origins of our current predicament. At this moment we can retroactively see the emerging disintegration of the compact that had been forged between labor, capital, and the state throughout the postwar decades; a pact that in many ways defined the extended period of sustained economic growth during this same era:

> During the period from 1945 to 1975 the product of economic activity was distributed through collective bargaining mechanisms, which, despite being hard to implement at times, were for the most part effective...[27]

And then, how this very disintegration eventually gave birth to the neoliberal age: the age of mass privatization, deregulation, planetary militarism, and the dominance of a financially-based global capitalism:

> ...That model, which was based on state and union mediation, was demolished. Redistributive capacity was brought to a halt and wiped out. Today, with the cancerous growth of finance, we've got a predatory capitalism, doomed to constant crisis because of its relentless headlong rush forward, driven by increasingly uncontrollable financial instruments.[28]

Perhaps the signature feature that can account for the difference in how the economy functions in the present versus how it operated prior to the neoliberal turn in the 1980s is in its relationship to financial markets. As economist Rana Forohoor has demonstrated, financial markets have become akin to a virus within the twenty-first century global economy; continually soaking up value from real production without reinvesting back into it:

> To understand how we got here, you have to understand the relationship between capital markets — meaning the financial system — and businesses. From the creation of a unified national bond and banking system in the U.S. in the late 1790s to the early 1970s, finance took individual and corporate savings and funneled them into productive enterprises, creating new jobs, new wealth, and ultimately, economic growth...

Over the past few decades, finance has turned away from this traditional role. Academic research shows that only a fraction of all the money washing around the financial markets these days actually makes it to Main Street businesses.[29]

In other words, the American economy has become successively *financialized* over the past decades. The national economy now orbits around globalized financial markets and complex monetary instruments as opposed to being grounded in the day to day economic life of industrial production, family farming, small businesses, and most importantly — local sensibility and local economies. Financial markets no longer work in concert and support the operation and growth of the productive business sector. Instead, they now have become a world unto themselves; subject to esoteric laws and complicated trading algorithms, and utterly divorced from the real-life struggles of ordinary global citizens.

Although this shift has been undoubtedly exasperated by ideological factors — a thorough reconditioning of our common sense thinking that has made us progressively devalue the importance of our public resources and spaces, collective bargaining, and social institutions for a thinking that centers more and more around personal identity, competition, and the ability of individuals to gain direct market access[30] — it is also a shift that has been deeply shaped by technology. The dawn of the neoliberal age can also be seen as the period in which a whole range of technologies — global networks, the digital medias, and a whole series of new productive technologies such as mass automation and the collection of big data — would be introduced into consumer markets and radically transform both the function and structure of the previous socioeconomic order: the shift from industrial to postindustrial capitalism in Western economies.[31]

The period of industrial capitalism dealt with, first and foremost, the intersection of mechanical modes of production and the labor performed by human bodies — as in the sweat of muscles performing work in the factory or on the docks of any major port city[32] (or in the case of the white-collar version, the organizational work model once favored by the mid-twentieth century American corporation: rows of cubicles and the figure of the "grey-suited man" who crunched his endless numbers day in and day out).[33] This was a period that was demarcated by the presence of large centralized institutions, hierarchical bureaucracies, and organized spaces of production.[34] What the election of Ronald Reagan can now be seen to have represented is simply the emerging breakdown, the impending implosion, of this very socioeconomic framework. Industrial-based capitalism could no longer operate in American society when exposed to both the ideological force of neoliberalism — individuality over solidarity; passive consumption in lieu of active citizenship — and the decentralizing power of networked technologies. The once centralized core functions of the office building or the assembly line have been outsourced to foreign shores while labor in the information age has become mobile, precarious, and scattered among individual global players.[35]

We can see this transformation most clearly in how the notion of work itself has been so thoroughly transformed in the past decades by the effects of neoliberalism: instead of using the worker's muscle it uses his or her brain; instead of using the sweat from the worker's brow it now uses the far limits of his or her emotional and creative potential; and instead of producing a range of serialized commodities on the assembly line it produces the flexible networks, the personalized advertising, and the simulated imagery central to the twenty-first century consumer experience.

But what has also been transformed is the very way in which work is *perceived*. In the era of industrial capitalism work was often viewed as a type of death sentence: a 9–5 shift that was regarded as fundamentally inhuman; a period of the day that was

23

barely tolerated by the worker in the factory or office building and was only performed in exchange for a set wage. Work was not glamorized; it was not seen as being a way to express one's creative potential.[36]

Today, however, that *perception* of labor has definitely changed. Because labor has become ever more specialized and fragmented in today's postindustrial economy, the worker more and more considers his job to be the most important part of his life: work has become ideologically reconstituted in the postindustrial economy as the signature place where one's emotional, creative, and intellectual potentials can be fully put to use. Today work is largely regarded as the place where one can most directly contribute to the betterment of society, which is almost the exact opposite of how work was perceived in the industrial era — where it was often seen as an alienating, exploitive exercise that was only tolerated for a wage.[37]

But there is another feature that can further describe the transformation of the perception of labor in the age of neoliberal globalization. That is, the fact that today virtually our entire range of experiences as human beings — our social, cultural, even our spiritual experiences[38] — are now comprehensively exposed to the logic of networked technologies. In other words, within our present era of postindustrial capitalism, both the forces of economic production and the majority of our social interactivity are more and more centered in the *virtual* sphere. What is thus depleted in this scenario — from the constant bombardment of content within our social media feeds, the precariousness of work when integrated into the flux of global networks — is, essentially, the "real world." One only needs to walk into a cafe in any major American city today to see this phenomenon clearly demonstrated: a coffee shop full of human bodies staring at their screens and communicating within the virtual realm in lieu of their immediate environment.

Our lives in the postindustrial era have been exponentially

transferred to the screen for two interrelated reasons. The first is that labor itself has ceased to be physical. It has ceased to be a formula of timed work shifts in which human bodies operate machinery or perform a set of repetitive duties within a hierarchical office bureaucracy. Work has now become an exercise of cognitive labor that is more and more focused on the specialized intellectual and creative capabilities of individualized information workers.[39] And, as a direct result of that shift, work for the individual becomes increasingly precarious, increasingly absent of any social protections such as long-term pensions and basic health care, while being increasingly deprived of its capacity to promote solidarity with other workers: contrary to the common assumption that in the digital era we are becoming ever more connected with each other; in actuality, we are retreating further and further into our private fantasies and our disconnected worlds.[40]

The second reason — as we have already mentioned being a direct result of the ideological effects of neoliberalism — is that the primary way the individual now asserts their identity, the primary way an individual now demonstrates his or her identity is through *work itself.* That is to say, because our community and civic life becomes increasingly barren, because our social relationships become more and more of a public spectacle designed to get likes and shares, the shift of our collective creative energies are transferred toward our ultra-personalized labor and individualized economic productivity: in the age of neoliberal globalization *work becomes our life and our life becomes work*:

...as the traditional world of work is integrated into networked technology, the boundaries between work life and personal life become indistinguishable; work space and work time are intermingled with their private, personal counterparts. These novelties allow workers to bring their personal, lifeworld qualities of creativity, intimate relationships, and deep personal engagement to bear on their work activities...[41]

Although it may seem on the surface that this shift (as opposed to the seemingly cold, rote labor on the assembly line) is a positive and progressive one, it is nevertheless proving to be not the case. When work becomes our entire identity, subject to market laws and abstract technological mediation, what then becomes of our flesh, our relationships, our home, and our local communities? One can only note that they become progressively deprived of their life affirming energy. And with that, any potential cultural and social activity not inscribed by the logic of global capitalism, and the objective power of networked technologies becomes increasingly difficult to produce and sustain.

So, in the neoliberal era we can thus see two distinct shifts that have been brought forth by the transformation of global capitalism since the Reagan years: *the financialization of the economy and the virtualization of our social and personal life.*

It is interesting to note that it is within *this* very socioeconomic transformation that Reality Television becomes a cultural phenomenon; where a medium such as Reality Television suddenly becomes so visible in our day to day lives. We are in a situation today where all forms of technology are progressing with such astonishing speed, where technology is becoming ever more animated and sentient, that it is leaving our actual lived experience increasingly fragmented, isolated, and empty: because our embodied experience in the "real world" becomes so boring and stagnant, it migrates to our television sets and to the screens of our various devices. Reality Television, live streaming, and 24/7 social media engagement thus become emblematic of our lives under the force of neoliberal globalization in the twenty-first century.

In a certain respect, with the premiere and subsequent wide success of *The Apprentice* in 2004, Donald Trump has become emblematic of this precise paradigmatic shift. *The Apprentice* was a watershed moment that can now be seen as a program that signifies the very transformation that we are thus far attempting to highlight: the migration of social life to the virtual realm and economic production to the financial realm. In other words, *Donald Trump himself is symbolic of this same collective transformation of our lives, our culture, and our economy.*

I think this is where people fundamentally underestimate Donald Trump: yes, he's boorish, crude, and often displays a shocking lack of policy acumen and sense of historical context when addressing the American public. But in terms of his purely intuitive understanding of the global media's progression in the age of digital networks and Reality Television, in his capacity to effectively grasp the evolution of the twenty-first century pop-cultural and political domain, he is nothing short of genius. It is without question that the phenomenal emergence of Reality Television and the wide success of *The Apprentice* dramatically elevated Trump's presence in American culture.[42] The endless circulation of his image and signature rhetorical memes — "You're fired!" — helped bring forth a scenario in which his phantasmagorical presence seemed to somehow always be lurking in the background of American culture.

But it is not only the fact that Donald Trump has grasped the ongoing metamorphosis of twenty-first century media practices far better than the national news outlets and the class of professional pundits that arrogantly dismissed his campaign from the very beginning; he can also be regarded as an archetypal symbol of the very metamorphosis he has so effortlessly comprehended: the very image of Trump is now indicative of our own era — the era of digital news feeds, unfettered global capitalism, and the emergent phenomenon of fake news.

But this very transformation, in which the cultural and political rise of Donald Trump bears witness too, is also emblematic of a deeper shift that is now bringing forth the makings of a new global order. It is an order in which the virtual takes precedence over the real, where financial capitalism displaces concrete forms of production, and where marketing, branding, and slogans become more important than the product or service they are attempting to sell.[43]

Donald Trump has understood from the very beginning of his career as a Manhattan real estate developer — and well before the emergence of the world wide web in the 1990s and the medium of Reality Television that followed shortly thereafter — the power of branding and the power of the image. Yes, it is true that Donald Trump is a real estate developer who oversees the transformation of "real" materials such as steel and concrete into skyscrapers and luxury hotels in cities across the globe. However, he is also well aware that today the most important feature of a newly constructed skyscraper's "reality" is not the steel or concrete, but rather the branding and imagery that it is associated with. In short: Donald Trump knows that the domain of the image, the realm of the sign, and the size of your net worth displayed upon a computer screen have come to be the all-important features of life in the era of postindustrial capitalism.

The transformation of capitalism from its industrial into its postindustrial phase has created the very conditions whereby a person like Donald Trump could become the leader of the free world. We have become a culture that is now educated through memes, soundbites, and digital news feeds. We are a population now enveloped by a sea of floating signifiers with no reference point other than the product or service they advertise. And our economy has become akin to a financialized planetary casino, severed from the concerns, needs, and realities of an embodied and localized humanity.

What must be minimally acknowledged, after taking into consideration how deeply this ongoing transformation has affected the very nature of humanity, is that Donald Trump may in fact only be a representation of the current socioeconomic paradigm that we have all found ourselves in in the twenty-first century.

In summary, by the time Ronald Reagan was elected in 1980 the deindustrialization of America that had taken place throughout the 1970s — a deindustrialization in which American based corporations abandoned the United States so to go abroad in search of cheap and deunionized labor — the national economy was well on its way to becoming primarily centered within the service, media, and financial sectors.

As labor became increasingly severed from the various protections and benefits once offered by union membership or long term employment for a single company, workers across the country were either laid off or forced to enter the precarious labor market central to the emergent neoliberal model.

The days of the set work shift that were symbolized by the time-card punching office worker or assembly line laborer were now largely gone, a cultural memory that was to now only exist within the American psyche. Neoliberal workers no longer had their pensions and generous insurance plans that were once protected and nurtured by postwar compact between the state, labor, and capital. Instead, the American worker suddenly became embedded into an entirely new model, a model in which the ideological terms deployed to justify such an arrangement were "flexibility," being part of an "open network," and becoming "innovative and creative" while on the job.

The predominant economic dynamism of today is thus a product of the long term historical development of capitalism itself. Although we continue to live in a society where competition and the ability to generate maximum profit are still the basic principles in how individuals and businesses orient themselves to the world, the Reagan years marked a turning point in how these same principles practically operated in our day to day experience: when secure employment from centralized corporations and manufacturing operations transformed into a model of individual entrepreneurship, a flexible labour market, and the technologically based lean business models that are now central to the neoliberal model.

There have been, of course, particular phases of this general development along the way. The 1990s, for example, gave birth to an array of new financial products on Wall Street, an intensification of telecommunication and online development, and the first dot com bubble. The first decade of the twenty-first century, up until the 2008 crash, was noted for the redirection of capital into the residential and commercial real estate markets and the trillion dollar bubble of the subprime mortgage market. And now, in the years after the post 2008 crash, globalized capitalism has focused more and more on technological based models such as Amazon, Uber, Alibaba, and other companies that operate as a platform offering an array of products and services.[44]

But not only has economic production largely migrated onto the global network and within a series of enclosed corporate platforms, so too has much of our cultural and social interactivity. And, from that very same shift that has taken hold of both contemporary American culture and global society at large, someone like Donald Trump — a person who recognized and mastered this developing trend long before most — was in a unique position to effectively *market* himself as the next President of the United States through the new media tools that this same digital transformation brought forth: Tweets, soundbites, and memes.

The discourses of Trump

We, as the citizens of America, are now joined in a great national effort to rebuild our country and restore its promise for all of our people. Together, we will determine the course of America and the world for many, many years to come. We will face challenges. We will confront hardships. But we will get the job done.[45]

Donald Trump, Inauguration Speech

There are five basic components that have thus far defined the overall political project of Donald Trump:

1. A rejection of illegal immigration and the subsequent desire to reassert the integrity of America's national borders.
2. In direct response to what he sees to be the most problematic features of neoliberal globalization — such as job outsourcing, free trade deals, and the ongoing deindustrialization of America's productive forces — his solution has been to mobilize a re-establishment of the industrial economy as the essential feature of American productivity: to bring back the coal miners, the factory workers, and laborers as the heart and soul of the national GDP. Meaning, that Trump sees no real problem with the increasingly problematic issues that are being produced by contemporary global capitalist dynamics; his intention is only to restore those dynamics into a nationalist framework, sealed and protected behind a metaphorical (and perhaps even literal if he fulfills his campaign promise) concrete wall.
3. To initiate a resurgence of national pride, national identity, and what he perceives to be the essential and undiluted historical purity of American culture.

4. A categorical rejection of identity politics and the key tenets of politically correct language.

5. A retreat into conspiracy theories, the utilization of social
media platforms such as Twitter to communicate important matters of governmental and foreign policy, and the
persistent charge of the mainstream media being a dis-
seminator of "fake news." Such instances all reflect the
breakdown of the general intellect, the public commons,
and political dignity in the information age.

2.1

One of the more infamous moments from the 2016 Presidential
campaign[46] was Trump's commentary regarding what he perceived to be the dire state of illegal immigration in America:

> When Mexico sends its people, they're not sending their
> best…They're sending people that have lots of problems and
> they're bringing those problems with us. They're bringing
> drugs. They're bringing crime. They're rapists. And some, I
> assume, are good people.[47]

What was evident in the aftermath of that public statement — a
series of news cycles that focused on the explicit racist content of
the speech — was the profound miscalculation of the professional pundit class in their analysis of Trump's remarks. Whereas
common wisdom would have assumed such a statement to be
nothing short of political suicide, a campaign-ending sound bite,
his words had the very opposite effect: a further mobilization
of his then developing political base and a subsequent rise in
his polling numbers. What was so underestimated by the professional class of Washington pundits and journalists was just
how frustrated a large percentage of Americans had become by
the unanswered questions and mounting problems regarding
the state of contemporary illegal immigration. The frustration

had grown to such a level that even commentary with clear and unmistakable racist overtones would be overlooked by a large percentage of the American population so long as the issue was being openly addressed.

The standard analysis of this development was that Trump supporters — "the basket of deplorables" in essence — were simply a xenophobic contingent of the American population and that Donald Trump was only tapping into a collective racism that was always-already there; a latent racism that was waiting in the wings to be mobilized into political action. Although it is undeniably true that a certain percentage of Trump supporters were in fact racist and gravitated to such rhetoric for that very reason, I think that such a collective assertion about the Trump political base is fundamentally misleading.

What if such an assertion was actually a strategy to displace and obfuscate other issues at hand; issues that were not only economically based, but ideological and structural that were then incorrectly diagnosed in purely cultural terms?

The fact of the matter is we cannot say exactly what the Trump Presidency fully means as of yet. But our speculation can only point to something where the convergence of celebrity, globalized capitalism, and the new media technologies central to neoliberalism intersect to form a peculiar kind of subjectivity that has been completely hollowed out of its positive content, and given over to a depoliticized logic of managing society — not through the specialists and technocrats as in the standard mode of neoliberal political management — but through the memes and Tweets and soundbites which endlessly circulate through the brain of contemporary American society so to create a kind of virtualized spectacle that reveals itself as populist fervor.

What is so fascinating about this arrangement — a truly revolutionary impulse if there ever was one — is that we seem to think this is just a new moment of American "populism" or a "reactionary" move of the American right so to restore something that has been irrecoverably lost. Although we can be sympathetic to this reading, it should ultimately be rejected: we are most certainly in new political territory now.

The militaristic and economic policies of Western powers over the past century throughout Latin America[48], Africa, and Asia are now finally seeing the fruits of their cumulative action: a mass exodus of poor migrants around the world now flooding into Western economies, desperate to escape their own ravaged lands. For the working- and middle-class Americans who are now watching and experiencing the effects of this migration — as their local communities are transformed before their eyes in under a decade from the effects of this migratory surge — it is creating not only a feeling of collective resentment toward the migrants, but also a sense of hopelessness, confusion, and anger that ultimately references their own deteriorating socioeconomic status.[49] And, that same sense of pervasive confusion and anger is further exacerbated by the very fact that they do *not* comprehend that the underlying dynamics driving this surge of immigration are actually deeply related to why their jobs have progressively disappeared, why opiates are ravaging their communities[50], and why much of middle America now feels a looming sense of cultural irrelevance in the era of twenty-first century globalization.

Donald Trump tapped directly into the deep reservoir of legitimate anger felt by the countless middle- and working-class Americans regarding the contemporary dynamics of illegal immigration: confusion as to its sociopolitical roots and fear as to its potential economic and cultural effects. However, rather than opening the possibility for a national dialogue regarding the militaristic and corporate roots of illegal immigration, a national dialogue that could show these migrants as human beings deserving of basic dignity and respect, Trump leveled the blame on the poor migrants themselves: a cowardly but predictable moment if there ever was one.

But beyond the unfiltered remarks by the then candidate Donald Trump against the individual Mexican migrants, what his rhetoric *appeared* to stand against was the destabilizing effects, the continual "liquification"[51] of social and political order that has now become a central feature to the ongoing project of neoliberal globalization. In other words, the synchronization of twenty-first century global capitalism with the de-centering effects of networked technologies — that which we can characterize as perhaps the core dynamic of neoliberal globalization — has entailed with it a continuous collapse of the majority of features that once defined the industrial-based, postwar economies of Western nations. American productivity has been largely outsourced to the sweatshops of the Third World; social interactivity, educational systems, and journalism have progressively migrated to the digital sphere; and national boundaries are now perceived as hindrances and obstacles to the efficient and optimal functioning of the global marketplace. This scenario — this permanent flux of markets, technologies, and people all with the purpose of generating maximum profit — is what we can effectively characterize as neoliberal globalization:

Globalization? The relocation of numerous sites of industrial production to countries with low labour costs and an authoritarian political regime? The transition during the 1980s in our old developed countries from an auto-centred economy, with a continual increase in workers' wages and social redistribution organized by the state and trade unions, to a liberal economy integrated into global trade and therefore export-orientated, specializing, privatizing profits, socializing risks and assuming a planetary increase in inequalities? A very rapid concentration of capital under the leadership of finance capital? The utilization of novel means whereby the velocity of circulation of capital initially, and of commodities subsequently, has significantly accelerated (generalization of air transport, universal telephony, financial machinery, the Internet, programmes geared to ensuring the success of instantaneous decisions, and so on)? The sophistication of speculation thanks to new derivative products and a subtle mathematics of risk combination? A spectacular decline of the peasantry, and the whole rural organization of society, in our countries?...A planetary struggle, sometimes muffled and sometimes of an extreme violence, to secure cheap access to raw materials and energy sources, particularly in Africa — continent of every variety of Western despoliation — and, consequently, atrocity? I know all this reasonably well, as in truth does everyone.[52]

But what Trump's definitive stance against the specter of illegal immigration now pouring across America's southern border speaks to is only his inability to coherently perceive and articulate that very problem. This is precisely why I stressed that Donald Trump *appeared* to articulate an authentic politics that rejected neoliberal globalization by standing firm against immigration: *Trump wants neoliberalism, absent the globalization.* What this means is that Trump wants all of the key features that are central to the basic operation of neoliberalism — the continued privatization of our public spaces, mass corporate deregulation and tax breaks for the wealthiest Americans,[53] promoting competition instead of the social protections and solidarity that could be offered by civic institutions and social welfare programs — but he only wants this parasitic and destructive system contained behind the protection of a wall, under the Stars and Stripes alone in which migrants are definitely excluded.

So for Trump, the problems that are now exploding to the surface in the neo-liberalized and globalized world are thus displaced onto the individual migrants — the poor migrants, the worst victims of this very system whose Latin American communities have been exponentially ravaged by global corporations in recent decades — that have made the harrowing decision to leave their home and attempt the southern border crossing. But in leveling the blame on the backs of the men, women, and children who have in fact illegally migrated to America, Trump is fundamentally unable to articulate this problem in its entire context; in its global context. He is unable, or perhaps unwilling, to see that unrestrained multinational corporate power — of which the Trump Corporation is absolutely a prime example — and exponentially increasing American militarism — of which Trump is an unabashed supporter — are intimately linked in an unfolding socioeconomic process that is chiefly responsible for the emerging crisis of mass planetary migration, a situation the Chinese artist and filmmaker Ai Weiwei calls "Human Flow."[54] This is a classic case of Donald Trump wanting to "have his cake and eat it too": one cannot support unrestrained global capitalism and American militarism and then completely disavow the human suffering and fallout that is produced as a result; a planetary suffering now lucidly represented in the ongoing global migrant crisis. Donald Trump has given voice to the countless working- and middle-class Americans who are, and rightfully so, deeply concerned and frustrated by the state of illegal immigration in contemporary America. They want and need a scapegoat to make sense of this extraordinarily complex issue. And that scapegoat has become, in the eyes of Donald Trump and his supporters, the poor migrants and the liberal politicians who have seemingly given them cover. But this dynamic is by no means an exclusively American situation. The migration of the Third World casualties resulting from Western militarism and multinational exploitation is now revealing itself in no uncertain terms across the globe:

"There is a nomadic proletariat that comes from the most devastated zones. This nomad proletariat is very strongly internationalized already, and spread across the whole earth. Many workers in Korea are Nepalese, or come from Bangladesh, just as a whole mass of workers here [in Europe] have come from Morocco or Mali."[55]

The now pervasive political rhetoric — whether it be Victor Orban in Hungary or Donald Trump in America — that refuses empathy and even more importantly refuses to understand and publicly acknowledge the sociopolitical roots of the global immigration crisis is a dangerous symptom of twenty-first century globalization. And it is symptomatic because such rhetoric is not the true root of the problem, it is rather what points to a much deeper pathology beneath the surface. The contemporary push to erect new border walls to stem the flow of the global refugee crisis, or the retreat to nationalistic fantasies about a fictitious past, can be seen as only that of strategies to systematically avoid confronting the heart of the problem in our contemporary world order.

2.2

There is an excellent scene in Jim Sheridan's 2016 film *Brooklyn* where the film's protagonist — a young Irish immigrant played by Saorise Ronan — is volunteering at a New York shelter serving Thanksgiving dinners to a group of down-on-their-luck men. As she is surveying the room, gazing at the collection of tragic and broken faces, a nearby Catholic priest says to her, "These are the men who built the bridges, the tunnels, the highways. God alone knows what they live on now."[56] It was a touching moment, and also a prescient commentary that foreshadows the future status of working-class men in American society: an expendable, forgettable, and ultimately unnecessary demographic in the emergent postindustrial economy of automation, artificial intelligence, and cognitive labor.[57] In many ways the rhetoric of Donald Trump has been specially directed toward this precise same demographic, directly speaking to the sense of deep loss that is now being produced from their cultural debasement. It was the working- and middle-class white men whom Trump identified as the "forgotten man" in the era of outsourcing and free trade, and Trump's entire campaign, the very core of his political rhetoric, was largely directed at this American demographic. The slogan, Make America Great Again, can be seen as the cat call that rallied this group into political mobilization.

One can only find incredible irony in the fact that the New Deal — one of the great and lasting achievements of the American left — was a politics that was once overwhelmingly supported by the parents and grandparents of this very same contingent: the various small farmers and workers of the Depression era who definitively sided with the Democratic party, the labor movement, and the various public investments initiated during this period over the interests of private capital in order to recover from the worst economic depression in American history:

> The Tennessee Valley Authority, the mega-hydroelectric programs in the West, and the Rural Electrification Administration brought power and higher living standards to the nation's backwaters. New financial regulations strengthened regional banks and held Wall Street in check.[58]

This is the legacy of the Democratic Party that it has largely (up until recent decades) been unconsciously associated with in the eyes of the American public: the party of the American worker, the party of social welfare, the party of equality, and the party that stood squarely against the interests of big business. The very fact that the globalized leftovers of the American working class would support a Manhattan billionaire and Reality Television star — who is symbolic of the very socioeconomic displacement which their grandparents and the legislative measures initiated by the New Deal stood squarely against — speaks in no uncertain terms about the seismic shifts in American politics in recent decades. And what this shift speaks to is by no means the fact that the populist-fundamentalism of Donald Trump has actually articulated a coherent vision that directly addresses the deep anxieties of working- and middle-class Americans. It is rather the fact that the remnants of the American working class have become so disenchanted by the policies of the contemporary Democratic party[59] — the party of FDR and JFK that was once their very backbone — that they have been reduced to a state of political apathy whereby the rhetoric of someone like Donald Trump, completely ungrounded, absent of a meaningful and orderly vision of global politics, suddenly becomes attractive. One cannot help but notice the presence of such a retroactive situation in contemporary American politics: that a Manhattan billionaire and member of the Republican Party was the only person able to speak directly to this now disintegrating political demographic. But how exactly did Trump construct this political bridge; that is to say, how was he able to gloss over the profound differences between himself and an unemployed coal miner in West Virginia or mechanic in Pennsylvania? All we can note is the fact of Trump's substantial personal charisma and his truly brilliant ability to use his rhetoric in a way that directly tapped into this emotional reservoir of cultural and political loss, while finding convenient scapegoats — immigrants, cultural progressives, kneeling football players — to effectively blame.

The central ideological call from Donald Trump was to "bring back American jobs, bring back the miners and factory workers as the mainstay of America's productive forces, terminate all free trade deals that don't privilege national interests; and then, build a wall to protect ourselves from the hostile outside world." In other words, to turn back the clock of time and resuscitate the industrial economy; to turn back the clock of time during which white men controlled and benefitted most from society; to turn back the clock of time when social media wasn't daily disrupting the flow of information from centralized sources of power. The problem with this strategy is that it is not only completely incoherent, but that it is simply not possible. Not only has the global economy transformed in such a profound way since the introduction of the internet and digital networks, but so have human beings and their consciousness of the world. Bringing back a system of wage labor organized around industrial production set within a nationalist framework is an absurd solution to deal with the very real problems that are now being brought to the surface in a globalized world.

It is both important and uncomfortable to recognize that Trump, for all of his faults, and regardless of the fact that he has largely abandoned the core features of his populist stance since becoming President,[60] was absolutely *correct* in pointing out that there was something gravely wrong with the state of America today. He was correct to note that America was "no longer great." This is something that the opposition to Trump could never quite stomach; they could never fully face the fact that Donald Trump was actually on to something, that he was tapping into a collective frustration that was completely legitimate. It is not entirely relevant that his solutions to this Problem were disastrous, that he wasn't able to articulate the Problem clearly, or even the fact that his Presidency may in fact make these same Problems even worse. What is ultimately relevant is the fact that it took a Reality Television star, a man with no prior political experience, to point out to the Washington political establishment that America was "no longer great" from the cumulative effects of neoliberal globalization.

What is most interesting here is how Trump does not in any way see his own role, his own symbolic function, in the 40 years and counting of deindustrialization of America's productive forces, the increasing fragmentation and hostility of America's political atmosphere, and the economic stagnation of working- and middle-class Americans that is now felt across the board. This is the true irony of the situation: it is people like Donald Trump — billionaires who have made their money through financial speculation and the rise of the global media — who are most responsible for the plight and frustrations of his core political base.

2.3

Deeply related to both the project of securing the southern border to keep at bay immigration from Mexico and Central America, and the project of resuscitating the industrial-based economy as a counter-measure to the deterritorializing force of globalization, is the attempt to bring forth a resurgence in national pride, patriotism, and a collective fidelity to American culture. This element may in fact be the most potentially dangerous of what I have highlighted as the five key discourses of Donald Trump. The danger lies not in the fact that having a sense of patriotism, a simple fidelity to one's own sociopolitical background and culture is problematic in itself. The problem is rather the fact that the "patriotism" articulated by Donald Trump has little to do with an authentic love for America and its multifaceted and complex history, as in a patriotism that can simultaneously love and be appropriately critical at the very same time. The brand of patriotism that Trump is demonstrating and encouraging is rather something that Alain Badiou has categorized as a "reactionary nihilism":[61] a false machismo and overblown gesture of patriotism that is actually grounded in a sense of hopelessness and impotence. And, to be sure, this type of political consciousness is produced in direct response to what can only be articulated as the "progressive nihilism"[62] that is central to neoliberal globalization: the relegation of planetary society to nothing but a multicultural consumerism.

What this means is that the nationalistic desire for new walls to be erected and for society to return to a more "traditional" way of life — a contemporary phenomenon not nearly unique to America and Donald Trump — is by no means a sign pointing to a renewed sense of national sovereignty, but rather that of a crystal-clear sign that references the increasing fragility and irrelevance of the nation-state itself:

> Rather than resurgent expressions of nation-state sovereignty, the new walls are icons of its erosion. While they may appear as hyperbolic tokens of such sovereignty, like all hyperbole, they reveal a tremulousness, vulnerability, dubiousness, or instability at the core of what they aim to express — qualities that are themselves antithetical to sovereignty and thus elements of its undoing.[63]

The sudden retreat to "nihilistic" nationalism being brought forth to the very center of global politics by the rhetoric of Donald Trump — no real positive content, largely defined by a reactionary nostalgia — is perhaps the absolute worst strategy to effectively respond to the other expression of nihilism that has become a central feature of the ongoing project of twenty-first century neoliberalism: two wrongs do not make a right as the old saying goes. Neoliberal globalization, in its essential function, has the goal of transforming the world into a singular "multicultural" marketplace: all social spaces and collective forms of identity, such as nation-states, are progressively stripped of their power, public resources, and ability to promote shared values and consciousness.[64] The effects of this contemporary process are proving themselves to be disastrous across the globe: ecologically, economically, and perhaps most especially psychologically. But what is perhaps most inherently dangerous to the "progressive nihilism" of neoliberal globalization is that of its obverse movement: the reactionary nihilism, as in the various emergences of populist-fundamentalism that are now popping up across the planet such as Donald Trump and which are being produced as a counter-measure.[65] But not only is this solution ethically catastrophic, but it creates an endless feedback loop with the very thing it opposes.

In the primitive worldview of Donald Trump, he has amazingly quite correctly located and expressed throughout his campaign the inherent "disaster" of what neoliberal globalization — such as the injustice that free trade deals have brought to local workers around the world[66] — has wrought on national economies and local sensibilities. Donald Trump, like the millions of Americans who agreed with him, intuitively knows that there is something profoundly wrong with the neoliberal project. The problem is that Donald Trump misdiagnoses the underlying causes of this phenomenon and then, as a recourse, invokes nationalistic delusions and retreats into fantasies of an invented past as a counter-measure.

The German theoretician Walter Benjamin once remarked, "Every rise of Fascism bears witness to a failed revolution."[67] This is perhaps the perfect summation that can explain Donald Trump's rise as a political phenomenon and why his nationalistic and divisive rhetoric was able to find a place in twenty-first century America political discourse: the absolute failure of the "revolution" of neoliberal globalization over the past four decades has led directly to its fundamentalist-populist counter-measure; a counter-measure perfectly represented in the politics of Donald Trump.

2.4

One of the defining features of twenty-first century global capitalism is its seeming inversion in relation to its predecessor, the era of the industrial economy. In the period of industrial capitalism, a whole range of activities were naturally assumed to be beyond the scope of economic production: interpersonal communication that transpired outside of the factory or the office building, intimate and personal relationships, civic and communal institutions. These, and more, were fundamentally social activities: they were relatively free from direct mediation by market and technological forces. What the industrial era principally engaged was the flesh of the worker: repetitive and rote body work performed in the factories, docks, or in any number of the union trades or civil services.[68] The body of the laborer was put to work, and hard work it was. However, what was not put to work throughout this era was the worker's brain; his or her very soul.[69] The "soul" was left to its own devices outside of the 9–5 shift.

In the postindustrial era, however, the need of the worker's flesh to perform labor has been all but discarded and the brain has now become the principal site of the economy's productive forces: cognitive labor in the financial, media, and technological fields are now the key professions of the present-day global workforce. However, this mass utilization of the twenty-first century information worker's psychological energies has often become too much for the contemporary individual to bear, and what is often left for many is a pervasive sense of exhaustion, angst, and depression. Under the force of this system, a system which fundamentally entails information overload from the constantly enforced encounter with digital space, the human brain simply cannot cope.[70]

What this means is that the individual's "soul" (or brain if you prefer) in our present era of postindustrial capitalism (unlike the era of industrial capitalism) is *not* left to its own devices outside of the work shift to spend time with family, to engage in civic duties, or to form new solidarities. What occurs instead for the contemporary worker is that their soul — his or her entire range of cognitive, emotional, and intersubjective functions — is now on call 24/7; and often to the point of psychic and emotional exhaustion. Amidst this situation — with an entire society in possession of a smartphone connected into the global network, and therefore always able to potentially perform labor — social life is in the process of disappearing from its truly public dimension; it recedes further and further into the sphere of strictly private market and technological relations.

In today's environment there is simply no more boundary that separates one's professional life from one's personal life: these two spheres of life have become nearly indistinguishable within the operative frame of contemporary global capitalism. And we should see this transformation as being a direct consequence of both the introduction of neoliberal ideology into society at large and the mobilization of an entire range of digital technologies that now comprise the core of global networks: the dangerous combination that we can refer to as the very crux of neoliberal globalization.

Central to the discourses of neoliberal globalization is the remaking of society — such as public institutions and services, local cultural production, interpersonal relations, even the flesh of our bodies — into a space of *competition* between both individual and corporate interests.[71] In the neoliberal worldview, there is simply no conception of public resources, genuine social solidarity between people, and socio-cultural forms that are truly free from direct mediation by market dynamics. From the effects of unconsciously adopting this worldview, from the effects of being immersed within this very ideological perspective, active citizens are turned into passive consumers, and society itself is turned into a collection of individuals at odds with one another.[72] The now infamous Margaret Thatcher comment perfectly encapsulates the moment when this very logic started to become normalized in Western societies:

> They are casting their problems at society. And, you know, there's no such thing as society. There are individual men and women and there are families. And no government can do anything except through people, and people must look after themselves first.[73]

Let us frame the situation at hand that we now face in the present: when we become isolated consumers who are now engaged in an all-out competition for employment, housing, and resources — when we are systematically stripped of our very social consciousness and the recognition that we are part of a human community with the potential to develop deep and meaningful solidarity and spiritual resonance — what happens, to put it in simplistic terms, is that we are always in danger of being offended by the Other. We become, on one hand, increasingly aggressive, misogynistic, and xenophobic; we retreat into nationalistic fantasies about a historical purity that has been lost and must now be reclaimed. Or, on the other hand, our traumatized subjectivity becomes constantly offended, in need of "safe spaces"[74] to be protected from ideas that do not correspond to our hyper-individualized sense of the world, while at the very same time becoming completely antagonistic to even the mention of any universal possibility. These two opposed positions constantly reinforce each other, strengthen each other's ideological resolve, and thus produce a deadlock that we are now seeing played out on college campuses across the country and within the national political arena.

But why do we now face such a circular and hostile dynamic in our public conversations and in the way we collectively address each other? Why are we suddenly in need of a politically correct code to structure our interpersonal interactions? For the very reason we have just outlined above: when we are systematically stripped of our social consciousness, when we are systematically stripped of our public resources and public spaces, when we are ideologically transformed into "pure identities," full of idiosyncrasies and unresolved traumas that require personalized recognition and specialized justice, we cease to be citizens who are part of a living and diverse society. Instead, we become consumers who are always-already offended by the Other's potential encroachment. We have become this way — this never-ending sparring between a pathological hyper-sensitivity and a pathological crudeness — because of our society's present-day anomie and social alienation, the now pervasive inability to form lasting social bonds. We are fast becoming a society of "weak ties"[75] in which social relationships are nothing but in service to strictly economic ends. But when human life becomes nothing but a business, literally, as it is for so many people in their adoption of the neoliberal worldview, we not only become hyper-individualistic and aggressive toward our own ends, but also hypersensitive to any perceived slights.

So what is truly ironic about Donald Trump's categorical rejection of "political correctness" — his near total dismissal of both the language that structures contemporary identity politics and the reason why it has become so necessary — is that he is representative of the very forces that have created the conditions for this type of discourse that now permeates American society, discourses that he now openly mocks and derides. In other words, political correctness is only made possible by the radical *individualization* of society that is fundamental to the project of neoliberalism. Case in point: when urban spaces are transformed from neighborhoods that once had distinct ethnic and working-class compositions into ones that only have expensive housing occupied by precarious and transient professionals — the process we call gentrification, the process that Donald Trump has made his billions from — a discernible result of this procedure is the *necessity* of politically correct language to serve as a protective measure to remedy the inconsistencies and antagonisms that define such a social transformation.[76]

Donald Trump wants us to "get tough" and stop being "snowflakes." In a certain respect, we can agree with him to a point. But what he can't see, what he can't fathom, is that the reason why modern day liberal society has become populated by "snowflakes" is because of the very system that people like him have actively produced and directly benefitted from throughout their careers. When public resources and public institutions progressively collapse as they have done over the past decades, what is left are only the fragmented and traumatized individuals trying to pick up the pieces while endlessly competing with each other within a system that claims that all resources are limited and finite: this is the tragic world that neoliberalism and people like Donald Trump have helped to bring to life and then have the audacity to engage in a critique that displaces the blame away from themselves.

2.5

If there is any lesson from the first year of the Trump administration, it is simply that the bar to civility can always be lowered: a true "race to the bottom" in the domain of public discourse. A case in point was the recent commentary at a ceremony honoring a group of Navajo wind talkers — the code breakers who were an integral part of the World War 2 national intelligence apparatus — when he made a ridiculously inappropriate reference to Massachusetts senator Elizabeth Warren's infamous nickname, Pocahontas.[77]

There is no point in even trying to legitimately critique this rhetoric, pointing out the level of degradation that such commentary brings to the symbolic dignity of the Presidency or how such a remark could potentially be deeply offensive to Native Americans: an exercise in futility if ever there was one in the age of smartphones and social media feeds. What may be more important to note is how these remarks by President Trump (and countless others) simply mirror the kind of off the cuff, casual style of language that you now routinely find on social media (or on city street corners, if people actually still conversed there). Amidst the cultural conditions of 2017 America, even being at an official White House ceremony no longer guarantees a certain level of symbolic dignity.[78]

It is all too easy to displace this ongoing collapse of basic manners in our society entirely onto Donald Trump, pointing out that his style of communication is setting a horrifying example for all Americans as they are made to endure his online temper tantrums and childish commentary. Although this is undoubtedly true, we must also realize that this kind of now prevalent public discourse — increasingly inappropriate, increasingly rude, increasingly lacking all semblance of basic civility — is precisely what you will get in a society where everyone has a Twitter feed and a smartphone in their hand: disembodied virtual communication, as a structural feature of itself, begets an endless erosion of basic manners and public decency.

So it is in fact an entirely justified position to be outraged at what can only seem like the daily tirades that are routinely disclosed on Donald Trump's Twitter feed: such as his childish rants directed at Tennessee senator Bob Corker, or his disturbing verbal sparring with North Korean leader Kim Jon Ung — to name only a couple of instances.[79] But what we have often failed to realize in our critical stance on Trump's rhetoric is that this is only the prototypical type of rhetoric that a medium like Twitter will eventually bring forth from anyone who uses it: an incremental lack of civility, a wholesale collapse of knowledge, and a dissociation from both the past and the future when fully immersed in the coordinates of digital real time. In other words, in our collective shock in the face of such un-Presidential behavior and rhetoric, we have not nearly engaged in a substantial critique of the *form* where this behavior emerges from and have instead focused entirely on the *content* instead: if we are to accurately read the cultural symbolism of Donald Trump we cannot displace the cause of this rhetoric and behavior entirely onto his moral deficiencies and personal lack of manners, as we must be willing to reflect his behavior into the contemporary state of culture itself; we must be willing to see his actions as symbolic of the disembodied society created by our new media environment.

And, to be sure, the increasingly disturbing communication that is now routinely found on Twitter and other social media sites is simply indicative of a much larger process taking hold, a process that is fundamentally altering human behavior and even our collective neurology as we become further enveloped into screen culture and global capitalist logic. From this dynamic, from the constant encounter with de-centered media content coupled with the ever-increasing imperative for the individual to be constantly innovative, productive, and creative in both their work and private life, the human brain simply:

> cracks. And it is actually cracking, collapsing under the stress of hyper-productivity. An epidemic of panic is spreading throughout the circuits of the social brain. An epidemic of depression is following the outbreak of panic. The crisis of the new economy at the beginning of the [twenty-first century] has to be seen as a consequence of this nervous breakdown.[80]

Is not Donald Trump's election the clearest proof imaginable that the social brain of our society is "cracking," that it is breaking down amidst the absolute onslaught of information overload, corporate surveillance, and personalized advertising in our contemporary age? Is not the fact that we elected a man like Donald Trump an indictment, not of the "basket of deplorables," but the structural conditions and ideological horizon of globalization and the unchecked proliferation of digital technologies into our lives, bodies, and brains?

One of the chief proselytizers of the digital revolution and information economy throughout the 1990s was the philosopher, theorist, and co-founder of *Wired* magazine Kevin Kelly. His 1995 book *Out of Control,* which is now regarded as one of the principal texts that forecast the rise of global networks, lucidly describes in the following passage the emergence of the networked economy into our social and cultural consciousness:

As very large webs penetrate the made world, we see the

first glimpses of what emerges from that net – machines that become alive, and evolve, a neo-biological civilization. There is a sense in which a global mind also emerges in a network culture. The global mind is the union of computer and nature, of telephones and human minds and more. It is a very large complexity of indeterminate shape governed by an invisible hand of its own. We humans will be unconscious of what the global mind ponders. This is not because we are not smart enough, but because the design of a mind does not allow the parts to understand the whole. The particular thoughts of the global mind – and its subsequent actions – will be out of our control and beyond our understanding.[81]

We should note how fundamentally correct Kelly was in his prediction that "the particular thoughts of the global mind will be out of our control and beyond our understanding." Isn't this forecast the precise scenario that we find ourselves in today? Isn't this forecast the actual state of affairs for the contemporary global order? The world of global technology and global capitalism is moving at such a pace while perpetually disrupting our psychic equilibrium that we are unable to grasp it and give to it a coherent and collective sense of meaning; we are fundamentally unable to effectively theorize it.

What is most interesting is how Kelly, who simply gives a specific voice to the general ideological trend, seems to look upon this looming inability to comprehend our world and our life as a positive thing, as "progress," rather than point it out for the true human catastrophe that it is.

The lesson here is that when the social, economic, and cultural processes that comprise a society start to move beyond its cognitive capacities, when society is unable to theorize these processes in any coherent way, *meaning is thus reduced to the level of individual interpretation and bare economic necessity*. Donald Trump's disturbing interpretation of politics, history, and economics — an interpretation that is often solely of his own limited perception, absent of any external reference point — is therefore *perfectly aligned* with the zeitgeist of our time. Donald Trump is not some alien intruder into our culture and political domain; he is simply par for the course of twenty-first century American society. He has emerged into our politics as a symbol that references a contemporary world order that has now gone "beyond our understanding," a political order which thus directly lends itself to his simplifications, generalizations, and continual debasement of public civility and common sense.

The charge of "fake news"[82] that is now mutually directed from either side of the political spectrum toward its perceived opponent — Democrats and Republicans; MSNBC and Fox News — completely misses the underlying dynamic that now structurally produces this phenomenon, a phenomenon that is completely independent of political affiliation. What we are ultimately dealing with in the sudden rise of fake news is only the collective reaction of the human psyche to the incredible power and indeterminacy of global networks that are actively transforming the consciousness, the neurological composition of the human mind, and how human beings give, receive, and process information: factual information that does not agree with our perception of the world is simply dismissed as "fake," while at the very same time an ocean of non-factual information and content is produced that conforms to our distorted individual perceptions. It is entirely disingenuous for liberal Democrats to lay the blame of "fake news" onto the feet of Donald Trump or Fox News. And in the precise same way it is entirely disingenuous for conservative Republican politicians to wax poetic about Trump's debasement of civility in the public sphere.[83] The fact of the matter is that Donald Trump is only symbolizing the actual state of affairs that we are now collectively immersed in: the extreme conditions brought forth from the cumulative effect of four decades of neoliberal globalization.

3

Trump and the resistance

I think a form of vitality remains in every human being, something irreducible that resists. I have to tell you, in fact, that if I weren't convinced that there's something in the human being that fights and resists, I'd quite simply have given up writing...I'm firmly of the belief that this particular, irreducible element (of humanity) can't be universalized or globalized, that it can't be part of some standard form of exchange. Will human beings do something positive with it one day? We can't say. The issue is by no means decided. And that, in fact, is where I find scope for optimism.[84]
Jean Baudrillard, From Hyperreality to Disappearance

The two pivotal events that defined the final leg of the 2016 Presidential race were the leaked Access Hollywood video in which Donald Trump was overheard speaking a string of the most outrageous vulgarities, and FBI director James Comey's announcement that he was re-opening the investigation into Hillary Clinton's use of a private email server during her tenure as Secretary of State in the Obama administration.[85]

The Access Hollywood video — a truly low moment in the history of American political discourse where even the appearance of civility was definitively vacated — that was released on September 17 appeared to be the final (of many potential finals) nail in the coffin for the Trump campaign. The polling numbers instantly reflected the shock of the tape's content, and even with Donald Trump issuing an immediate public apology for his remarks, Hillary Clinton's victory now appeared imminent. But even in the face of an apparently now certain defeat, Trump nevertheless persisted against all odds. Almost immediately after the release of his taped apology, his rhetoric increasingly focused on both the character deficiencies of Hillary Clinton and the problematic sexual history of her husband, whom Trump unabashedly referred to as "a rapist."

And then, the unthinkable: in perhaps one of the most pivotal moments of any Presidential campaign in American history, FBI director James Comey announced that he was — after being informed of the possibility of potentially incriminating information discovered on the confiscated laptop of former US Congressman Anthony Weiner — re-opening the investigation into Hillary Clinton's private email server. The announcement immediately energized the Trump campaign while dramatically bringing to the surface the profound skepticism that the American public already had regarding the integrity and character of Hillary Clinton. And no matter that James Comey announced only two weeks later that there was in fact no incriminating evidence discovered to warrant any further investigation into Clinton's tenure at the State Department; the reality of a Trump presidency was officially born.[86]

Yes, it was debated by pundits across the political spectrum. Yes, it was mathematically hypothesized by the sophisticated algorithms deployed by pollsters. And yes, it was dreamt about every night throughout Trump-land. But even with all of the mounting speculation, it nevertheless seemed as if no one *really* believed that a former Reality Television star and New York City property developer could be the next leader of the free world — until election night.

I can still vividly recall the shock on the faces, the authentic sense of disbelief in my own experience, when the final numbers from Florida were officially tallied. And then North Carolina. And Wisconsin. Pennsylvania. In many ways, the mass mobilization of the Democratic Party, the national mainstream media, and countless individuals across the country into a state of permanent resistance to the Trump presidency was greatly intensified by the genuine sense of shock felt on election night;

the lingering sense that a profound and unimaginable injustice had occurred that evening. And what followed that collective shock, now articulated in a singular word, which encapsulates the broad and absolute coalition of opposition to Trump and his politics, is *Resistance.*

But, what exactly does this politics of resistance center around? What foundation is its project constructed upon? What are its ultimate goals?

Perhaps the true irony of the widespread resistance to Donald Trump is the fact that it is not, as it were, resistance in the truest sense of the word; as in a force that is actively undermining an entrenched system of power so to bring forth something new. This is not to take anything away from the individuals and organizations across the country who have very real and legitimate concerns about Trump and feel themselves to be engaging in authentic acts of resistance. But in another sense, in a sense that sees this resistance in the broadest sense, we could make the provocative claim that the now pervasive resistance to Trump is actually more akin to a reactionary gesture; an attempt to reconstitute the status quo of the more palpable and acceptable neoliberal policies.

But why is this the case? And, furthermore, why are the resistors of Trump not even aware of this feature of their engagement?

The politics of Donald Trump was grounded and articulated in a fundamentalist-populist reaction against the discourses of what we could classify as the mainstream liberal-democratic order and the general dynamism of neoliberal globalization. Trump's policies and rhetoric are not simply a rejection of the American Democratic Party; they were that which *resisted* the basic framework of the liberal-democratic order as such: the discourses of multicultural globalization, the utilization of politically correct language to mediate public commentary, the logic of unrestricted free trade and outsourcing, and the ongoing dissolution of national identity and national boundaries for an emergent global society. What we had with the emergence of Trump — and along with European politicians such as Marie Le Pen in France and Nigel Farage in Great Britain — was a fundamentalist-populist reaction, *a resistance* to the near hegemony of the global liberal-democratic order and their neoliberal practices:

> By undercutting social solidarities and destroying ecological equilibriums, the neoliberal program of accelerated capital expansion immediately spawned its neoconservative shadow in the form of a military, moral, and religious return to order. Nothing could have made better cover for the denial of democratic critique, the clampdown on civil liberties, and the continuing budgetary shift from social welfare to corporate security. The backlash against globalization became a powerful new tool of manipulation, used by the same elites who launched the whole process in the first place.[87]

When taking into account the above passage, a passage that summarizes the intertwined political relationship between neoliberalism and its populist shadow, one can only note the irony of the situation we now find in the current resistance to Trump: that the current resistance by the mainstream liberal-democratic order to Trump is only that of a resistance *to resistance itself*. This is what liberals cannot quite face up to, cannot quite bear to fully digest: that it was Trump and his followers who were the ones who engaged in the true act of resistance. The problem is that the liberal worldview is now stuck in a mode of discourse and critique that perceives the state world as it was in the 1950s: when white men held absolute power over the socioeconomic domain; when the nuclear, heteronormative family was still fully in tact; when the voices of women and minorities were definitely excluded from public discourse. This is an exceedingly sensitive topic and we should by no means discount the historical trauma that has not nearly been addressed and resolved. But, nevertheless, one can only note that we do not, by any means, still live in such a world often articulated by the standard liberal critique. The whole point of the rise of Trump is the attempt to recapture that world *for the very reason that it no longer exists.*

In other words, the rise of neoconservatism in the 1990s and the early 2000s, now followed by Trump's brand of populist-fundamentalism (a direct evolution and radicalization of core neoconservative logic), is essentially that which "resists" some of the core discourses and tenets of the neoliberal project; discourses that have progressively undermined and even mocked this very way of life.

What ultimately has to be recognized in this scenario — in witnessing this never-ending back and forth between two political ideologies and ways of life that desperately present themselves as unrelated and ideologically opposed — is that we are simply dealing with two sides of the very same coin: the positive content of twenty-first century neoliberal globalization and its negation; its fundamentalist-populist shadow. What we are ultimately dealing with are two sides of a coin that are equally trapped and hamstrung, albeit in entirely different ways, by the same underlying logic of twenty-first century global capitalism.

So what is desperately missing in this situation is a new kind of thinking that seeks to address the functioning of the *coin itself;* a kind of thinking and political awareness that can effectively respond with clarity, dignity, and strength to what both Donald Trump *and* Hillary Clinton signified in their combined *and* opposed political positions in the 2016 Presidential election. But what can we do to effectively respond to this dynamic? There are no easy answers here, and I am most certainly not in possession of any groundbreaking ideas that could serve as an alternative possibility. Perhaps what must first happen, before any positive project is articulated, is simply to take honest stock of what is here now; to bring forth an analysis of the present situation that can be relayed to everyday people in common sense terms, divorced from old alliances and ideologies. It is important to recognize how the system that we are now part of actively encourages us "to do something," "to make our voices heard," and "to take action" regarding the state of the world. It constantly prescribes manic activity; it applauds us when we erupt in anger and outrage to any social media headline that does not match our individualized perceptions, and tells us we must immediately protest against any and all signs of what it deems to be oppression. But what the system doesn't encourage, what it nearly forbids actually, is patient reflection, measured and straight forward discourse, and a worldview that is grounded in basic common sense and universal decency. The eruption of "resistance" that emerged in the weeks following the election of Trump — an intensity of resistance that has since largely dissipated — spoke to this sense of looming panic that is now daily induced within the global population; this sense that we must immediately "do something" so we can avoid actually thinking about the situation itself.[88]

To effectively push back against Donald Trump and his politics today, what must occur is not necessarily direct action, but rather direct thought. Before it is possible to effectively act it is first essential to step back from engagement and take sufficient time to reflect upon what it is we are actually resisting, and what it is we actually want to bring forth a better world for humanity:

A critical analysis of the present global constellation – one which offers no clear solution, no practical advice on what to do, and provides no light at the end of the tunnel, since one is well aware that this light might belong to a train crashing towards us – usually meets with reproach: "Do you mean we should do nothing? Just sit and wait?" One should gather the courage to answer: "YES, precisely that." There are situations when the only true practical thing to do is to resist the temptation to engage immediately and to "wait and see" by means of a patient, critical analysis. Engagement seems to exert its pressure on us from all directions.[89]

With everything happening today at such a high velocity — as the dynamics of our politics, technologies, and global economy seem to be transforming daily — the completely natural urge is to "resist," to "take action" in order to arrest the situation before our sense of helplessness and panic gets any worse. But what we also must account for is the often unnoticed fact that the pervasive urge to "resist" is actually part and parcel of the very ideology that we are in fact desiring to escape from.

To truly change politics in contemporary America, the true strategy of resistance may actually be *to think*.[90] And not only to think in a refined, theoretical sense; but also in a way to bring forth a resurgence of common sense wisdom that is now so desperately needed in both our political and public conversations.[91]

In Donald Trump's book *Time to Get Tough: Making America #1 Again*, he states forthrightly what he feels to be the proper diagnosis for the inertia of contemporary American politics:

Restoring American wealth will require that we get tough. The next president must understand that America's business is business. We need a president who knows how to get things done, who can keep America strong, safe, and free, and who can negotiate deals that benefit America, not the countries on the other side of the table. A president doesn't 'create' jobs, only businesses can do that. But he can help create an environment that allows the rest of us — entrepreneurs, small businessmen, big businessmen — to make America rich. The damage that Democrats, weak Republicans, and this disaster of a president have inflicted on America has put us in a mess like we've never before seen in our lifetimes. To fix the problem we've got to be smart and get tough. But there is reason for optimism. We are Americans. We have the potential, we just need the right leadership. Let's Make America Great Again![92]

We should all unconditionally agree with Donald Trump here: yes, let's Make America Great Again; but with just one caveat: *just not the way you want to.*

By all accounts it seems that we are quickly rushing toward an inflection point in the unfolding of the American story: will our country be swallowed whole by the techno-capitalism being furiously unleashed by Wall Street and Silicon Valley, a metastasizing and multiplying force that is now spawning division and strife across American society nearly every day, given cover by the media as its causes are displaced to anyone and anything that can suit for the next news cycle; or, will a new politics emerge that can re-symbolize what it even means to be American and save us from ourselves?

I don't particularly like to make such definitive statements, but I believe this may in fact be the only question that matters today: *All others pale in comparison.*

Epilogue

The people no longer exist, or not yet...the people are missing.
Giles Deleuze

In Jose Saramago's novel *The Cave* he tells the story of Cipriano Algor, a traditional potter who lives an otherwise quiet life in the countryside and sells his artistry directly to a megaplex — a housing complex, shopping mall, and planned city all rolled into one — called The Center. After having developed a long-term but frustrating business relationship with The Center, its buying department informs Cipriano that they are no longer in need of his pottery; that the market has changed and consumers are not interested in purchasing folk pottery such as his any longer. Facing an impending financial crisis because he will be unable to carry on in his life as a potter without his principal buyer, Cipriano is reluctantly forced to move from his rustic countryside home into a small apartment in The Center with his daughter and son-in-law. But not long after moving to The Center and hearing rumors about a secretive dig occurring beneath its foundation, Cipriano decides to take it upon himself to investigate the subterranean situation. And what he discovers buried deep beneath The Center is none other than Plato's Cave itself. Saramago plays with numerous themes throughout his work: the country versus the city; contemporary consumerism versus traditional artistry; and the ongoing collapse of the family structure and local sensibility in the face of an abstract, impersonal way of life that is represented by The Center. But all of these interrelated themes ultimately point toward a singular realization at the novel's conclusion: that humanity has now found itself living within a globalized version of Plato's Cave. Entranced by the proliferation and multiplication of digital content, blinded by the ideological axioms of neoliberalism, and transformed into apolitical bodies versus active and engaged citizens, humanity has become like the prisoners chained to the wall in Plato's allegory: unable to see the world clearly any longer, we instead mistake shadows for reality and fleeting representations for the actuality of the world.[93] We now think of ourselves as the vanguards of the human race — the cumulative result of a highly progressive and dynamic biological and cultural evolution that has mastered the sciences, arts, and applied technologies — when in truth it rather seems we are descending into a new kind of barbarism and collective ignorance.

Was not the election of Donald Trump symbolic of this very same scenario? A political moment in which we elected a digital shadow, a virtual avatar to lead us into an uncertain future, and then adamantly refused to take any real responsibility for its causation; to refuse to see the chains that now entrap us?

But what is it exactly about our inability to coherently analyze political and social life that is now produced amidst the seemingly absolute horizon of social media feeds and a capitalist logic? Are we simply just in a process of losing touch with reality, as in the prisoners of Plato's Cave, and descending into a world of fantasy, "alternative facts," and click bait internet sites? On a certain level, this is certainly what it seems like: the now pervasive and eerie sense that reality itself is in the process of decomposing before our eyes into a sea of advertising images, corporate branding, fake news, and meaningless slogans.

But on a different level, what we are also losing today is not simply the cold, hard "reality" of our lived experience, but also the collapse of the *symbolic* order itself.[94] In other words, what we are now seeing emerge in the new global order is an increasingly rapid descent into aggressive, pseudo-Darwinian behavior that is ideologically reshaping the planet into one big "dog eat dog" world: a cold, hard reality of economic logic and technological mediation absent of the protection of social norms, cultural narratives, local communities, and the symbolic efficiency that has always been responsible for maintaining at least the appearance of civil human relations. Donald Trump's Twitter feed is just mirroring the world we now live in: brutally "real" commentary on everything and anything that corresponds to a purely egocentric economic expression designed to get likes and shares, absent of any awareness that one is part of a social-symbolic order. This is precisely what the late theorist Mark Fisher said in his reference to the contemporary world order being akin to "Capitalist Realism" — the only game in town — in the following passage:

> Capitalism is what is left when beliefs have collapsed at the level of ritual or symbolic elaboration, and all that is left is the consumer-spectator, trudging through the ruins and relics.[95]

Donald Trump is not the President of a country full of citizens who are aware of their mutual history, who feel part of both a unique local community and a broader global community, or who see themselves as simply small components of a much larger collective story taking place. On the far contrary, he is the President of a country full of individuated "consumer-spectators" — a collection of traumatized and disconnected individuals who see themselves and their small lives as supremely important, a national population that has been progressively severed from both their local communities and sense of shared national history, and a country that has been stripped from its economic autonomy and public resources by a globalized system that is now entirely focused on unbridled innovation and private competition. As Fisher notes above, what we now have in common is only our — whether we are aware of it or not — mutual participation, our full immersion, in a global capitalist marketplace. *And we are now paying the consequences.*

But even with this ongoing descent into the neoliberal abyss, I would nevertheless like to end here with a message of hope; a message that seeks to view Donald Trump's political ascension as that of an opportunity to reflect on our past, challenge our fixed assumptions, and perhaps even to open up the possibility for a new kind of politics to come forth in both American and global society. Such possibilities are, potentially, *the true meaning of Trump*: a proverbial "message from the gods" prompting us to open our eyes and take a clear look at the world we live in so to change our ways before we are simply overwhelmed to the point of no return from the now rapidly developing integration of computational technologies and globalized capitalism. In other words, we should adamantly resist the now pervasive call "to look within ourselves" so to only transform our individual psychic terrains and personal stereotypes. We must instead use this raw material within our collective psyche to "look without" and begin to actually address the economic and social systems that are now deteriorating before our eyes.

Zizek has often used throughout his writing the line from the Irish playwright Samuel Beckett so to explain the eternal dream for justice and equality, "Ever tried. Ever failed. No matter. Try again. Fail again. Fail better."

What is only clear today after reading the above line and reflecting on our current political dynamic is simply that we have failed, utterly, as a country in the most egregious of ways in both our political and civic duties. We have failed to protect our local communities and local cultures. We have failed to offer any real hope of a decent and dignified life to a whole new generation of young Americans. And perhaps most importantly we have failed to speak truth to Power, and to live in truth in our own lives.

So now, it seems what we must do as Americans, to follow Beckett via Zizek, is simply to "fail better." The solution is no longer to run into the future with a blind faith in the enduring goodness of progress. Now it seems the task is to rather look back and remedy our wrongs, correct the past as best we can, and speak again about a renewed America, and a new kind of global society. We will undoubtedly fail again in our quest, this is most certain. But we can *fail better* than we have before, we can strive to make slow and steady improvements; and we can struggle together before it's too late.

About the author

Brian Francis Culkin is a writer and film director. His previous books include *Postscript on Boxing, There is no such thing as Boston,* and *Conversations on Gentrification.* He has also written and directed two documentary films — *The Mission* and *Voices.* He graduated from Skidmore College in New York with a degree in American Studies and was a standout student-athlete, graduating as the all-time leading scorer in the basketball program. He is currently working on several projects including his first novel.

His website is www.brianculkin.com

Endnotes

Introduction/ The meaning of Trump

1. Berardi, F. (2017). *Futurability: the age of impotence and the horizon of possibility*. Brooklyn: Verso Books. Kindle Edition, Location 2831.
2. Kelly, K. (2017). *The inevitable: understanding the 12 technological forces that will shape our future*. New York, NY: Penguin USA, pp. 7-8.
3. In the same place, pp. 87-88.
4. Dionne, E. J., Ornstein, N. J., and Mann, T. E. (2017). *One nation after Trump: a guide for the perplexed, the disillusioned, the desperate, and the not-yet deported*. New York: St. Martins Press. See chapter 5,"Phony Friend of the Working Class."
5. Zizek, S. (2014). *The universal exception*. London: Bloomsbury, p. 197.
6. Kelly, K. (2017). *The inevitable: understanding the 12 technological forces that will shape our future*. New York, NY: Penguin USA, pp. 87-88.
7. Spence, L. (2015). *Knocking the hustle: against the neoliberal turn in black politics*. Brooklyn, NY: Punctum. Kindle Edition, p. 2.
8. Andersen, K. (2017). *Fantasyland: how America went haywire: a 500-year history*. New York: Random House, p.5. Andersen states here,"The American experiment, the original embodiment of the great Enlightenment ideas of intellectual freedom, every individual free to believe anything she wishes, has metastasized out of control. From the start, our ultra individualism was attached to epic dreams, sometimes epic fantasies – every American one of God's chosen people building a custom made utopia, each of us free to reinvent himself by imagination and will. In America, those more exciting parts of the Enlightenment idea have swamped the

sober, rational, and empirical parts."

9.   See, Berardi, F., Genosko, G., and Thoburn, N. (2011). *After the future*. Edinburgh: AK Press.

10. Chomsky, N. (2016). *Who rules the world?* New York: Metropolitan Books. See chapter 23,"Masters of Mankind."

11. For instance see, Spencer, H., and Stolberg, S. G. (2017, August 11). White Nationalists March on University of Virginia. Retrieved October 29, 2017, from https://www.nytimes.com/2017/08/11/us/white-nationalists-rally-charlottesville-virginia.html

12. See, Zizek, S. (2008). *For they know not what they do: enjoyment as a political factor*. London: Verso.

13. Trejos, N. (2017, June 07). Trump Hotels to start new mid-scale brand. Retrieved October 26, 2017, from https://www.usatoday.com/story/travel/roadwarriorvoices/2017/06/06/trump-hotels-start-new-mid-scale-brand/102559286/

14. Gandel, S. (2016, September 27). Trump Says NAFTA Was the Worst Trade Deal the U.S. Ever Signed (n.d.). Retrieved August 3, 2017, from http://fortune.com/2016/09/27/presidential-debate-nafta-agreement/

15. For instance, see Walmart Closes Stores, Leaving Small Towns with No Groceries (n.d.). Retrieved October 26, 2017, from http://time.com/money/4192512/walmart-stores-closing-small-towns/

16. Berry, W. (2016). *Our only world: ten essays*. Berkeley, CA: Counterpoint. Kindle Edition, pp. 55-56. Berry speaks at length about how one's"job" in an industrialized economy is spoken about in a completely abstract, near mathematical way – completely divorced from the actual work, or quality, of a human being's daily labor. He states,"This word, as we now use it in political cliches such as 'job creation,' entirely dissociates the idea of work from any idea of calling or vocation or vocational choice. A 'job' exists without reference to anybody in particular or any place in particular. If

a person loses a 'job' in Eastern Kentucky and finds a 'job' in Alabama, then he has ceased to be 'unemployed' and has become 'employed,' it does not matter who the person is or what or where the 'job' is. 'Employment' in a 'job' completely satisfies the social aim of the industrial economy and its industrial government."

17. Berry, W. (2016). *Our only world: ten essays*. Berkeley, CA: Counterpoint. Kindle Edition, See chapter 6, "Caught in the Middle", pp. 73-96.

18. Zizek, S. (2016). *Against the double blackmail: refugees, terror and other troubles with the neighbours*. London: Penguin Books, pp. 1-9.

19. Fisher, E. (2013). *Media and new capitalism in the digital age: the spirit of networks*. Basingstoke: Palgrave Macmillan. See chapter 3, "Network Market."

20. Berardi, F. (2017). *Futurability: the age of impotence and the horizon of possibility*. Brooklyn: Verso Books. Kindle Edition, Locations 253-392.

21. Frances, A. (2017). *Twilight of American sanity: a psychiatrist analyzes the age of Trump*. New York: HarperCollins, pp. 1-7.

22. Atkins, D. (2017, July 7). It Was Prejudice. It Was Economics. It Was Both. Retrieved September 3, 2017, from http://prospect.org/article/it-was-prejudice-it-was-economics-it-was-both

23. For instance, see Sykes, C. (2017, October 16). How the right lost its mind, sold its soul and embraced Donald Trump. Retrieved December 29, 2017, from http://www.newsweek.com/2017/09/29/right-lost-mind-embraced-donald-trump-668180.html

24. Berardi, F. (2017). *Futurability: the age of impotence and the horizon of possibility*. Brooklyn: Verso Books. Kindle Edition, Location 632.

Chapter 1

25. Berry, W. (2010). *What are people for?: essays*. Berkeley, CA: Counterpoint. Kindle Edition, p. 133.
26. Berry, W. (2016). *Our only world: Ten Essays*. Berkeley, CA: Counterpoint. Kindle Edition, p. 10.
27. Badiou, A., Gauchet, M., Duru, M., Legros, M., and Spitzer, S. (2016). *What is to be done?: a dialogue on communism, capitalism, and the future of democracy*. Cambridge: Polity. Kindle Edition, p. 82.
28. In the same place.
29. American Capitalism's Great Crisis and How to Fix It. (n.d.). Retrieved January 1, 2017, from http://time.com/4327419/american-capitalisms-great-crisis/
30. Harvey, D. (2005). *A brief history of neoliberalism*. Oxford: Oxford University Press. Kindle Edition, pp. 2-4.
31. Fisher, M. (2010). *Capitalist realism: is there no alternative?* Winchester, UK: Zero Books. Kindle Edition. See chapter 5, October 6, 1979: "Don't let yourself get attached to anything."
32. Rotella, C. (2004). *Good with their hands: boxers, bluesmen, and other characters from the Rust Belt*. Berkeley, CA: University of California Press, pp. 6-7, 23-25.
33. We should also remember that America, with its Jeffersonian origins, was also an economy that was centered around local economies and local farming. This rural mode of economic production differentiates itself from both industrial and postindustrial capitalism.
34. Deleuze, G. (1990). Postscript on Societies of Control. *L'Autre Journal*, no. 1 (May 1990).
35. Aranda, J., and Diederichsen, D. (2011). *Are you working too much?: post-Fordism, precarity, and the labor of art*. Berlin: Sternberg Press. Kindle Edition, Location 1774-1801.
36. Berardi, F. (2009). *The soul at work*. South Pasadena: Semiotext(e), pp. 76-77.

37. In the same place.
38. Exemplary here is the fact that neoliberal globalization has not only turned our bodies into organs of capital circulation, but also the fact that it is colonizing what we could call our spiritual experience through neoliberal ideologues such as Tony Robbins, Gary Vee, and Brendon Burchard. The point here is not to criticize these people as malicious individuals (which I don't believe they are by any stretch) but rather to see their presence as softening the blow of neoliberal ideology. For instance, see, Burchard, B. (2017). *High performance habits: how extraordinary people become that way.* Carlsbad: Hay House, Inc.
39. This is not to say that labor does not still run, at least hypothetically, along"shifts"today. The point is rather the fact that in the contemporary environment of "immaterial" labor that performs its work online – where industrial, clocked time is entirely irrelevant – work happens in a much more fluid, mentally centered, non-temporal way.
40. Williams, A., and Snricek, N. (2015). *Inventing the future: postcapitalism and a world without work.* Brooklyn: Verso, Location 1225-1232.
41. Fisher, E. (2013). *Media and new capitalism in the digital age: the spirit of networks.* Basingstoke: Palgrave Macmillan, p. 6.
42. Fisher, M. (2016, January 27). Donald Trump ignored his agent and did reality TV. It changed everything. Retrieved March 1, 2017, from http://www.washingtonpost.com/sf/national/2016/01/27/deciders-trump/?utm_term=.346f3f803fc5
43. Ebert, J. D. (2011). *The new media invasion: digital technologies and the world they unmake.* Jefferson, NC: McFarland & Co., Inc.
44. Srnicek, N. (2017). *Platform capitalism.* Cambridge, UK: Polity. Kindle Edition. Location 469-477.

Chapter 2

45. The Inaugural Address (n.d.). Retrieved August 1, 2017, from https://www.whitehouse.gov/briefings-statements/the -inaugural-address/

46. He technically made these remarks in 2015 just after he had announced he would be running in the 2016 election.

47. Posted by Ian Schwartz on June 16, 2015. Trump: Mexico Not Sending Us Their Best; Criminals, Drug Dealers And Rapists Are Crossing Border. Retrieved January 11, 2017, from https://www.realclearpolitics.com/video/2015/06/16/ trump_mexico_not_sending_us_their_best_criminals_ drug_dealers_and_rapists_are_crossing_border.html

48. For example, see Galeano, E. (2009). *Open veins of Latin America: five centuries of the pillage of a continent.* London: Profile Books, pp. 205-208.

49. Linskey, A. (2016, September 10) Being white, and a minority, in Georgia – The Boston Globe. Retrieved September 10, 2016, from https://www.bostonglobe.com/news/ nation/2016/09/10/being-white-and-minority-georgia/PpBh-8303fUVlfkYUDgQeuN/story.html

50. Culkin, B. (2017). *There is no such thing as Boston: gentrification and the disappearance of a city.* Charleston: Create Space. See chapter 4,"From Oxycontin to Heroin."

51. Bauman, Z. (2007). *Liquid times: living in an age of uncertainty.* Cambridge: Polity Press, p. 1. Bauman states here, summarizing the general conditions of contemporary globalization: "First of all, the passage from the 'solid' to a 'liquid' phase of modernity: that is, into a condition in which social forms... can no longer (and are not expected) to keep their shape for long, because they decompose and melt faster than the time it takes to cast them, and once they are cast for them to set. Forms, whether already present, or only adumbrated, are unlikely to be given enough time to solidify, and cannot serve as frames of reference for human actions and long

term strategies."

52. Badiou, A. (2012). *The rebirth of history*. London: Verso, pp. 9-10.

53. Hoxie, J. (2017, November 3). Trump's Tax Cuts Are the Biggest Wealth Grab in Modern History. Retrieved November 3, 2017, from http://fortune.com/2017/11/03/trump-gop-tax-plan-cuts-2017/

54. Bradshaw, P. (2017, December 07). Human Flow review – Ai Weiwei surveys shocking plight of migrants on the move | Peter Bradshaw's film of the week. Retrieved December 9, 2017, from https://www.theguardian.com/film/2017/dec/07/human-flow-review-ai-weiwei-migration-documentary

55. Badiou, A. (2016). *Our wound is not so recent: thinking the Paris killings of 13 November*. Malden, MA: Polity Press. Kindle Edition, Location 743.

56. See, *Brooklyn*, Jim Sheridan. BBC Films, 2016.

57. The White Working Class. (2017, June 01). Retrieved June 01, 2017, from http://prospect.org/article/white-working-class

58. Myerson, H. (2017, June 22). Place Matters. Retrieved June 22, 2017, from http://prospect.org/article/place-matters

59. Tibbets, J. (2016, November 20) This Is How The Democrats Betrayed The Working Class. Retrieved December 6, 2017, from https://thepavlovictoday.com/naked-opinion/democrats-betrayed-working-class/

60. Thompson, D. (2017, March 23). Trump's Populist Mirage. Retrieved June 04, 2017, from https://www.theatlantic.com/business/archive/2017/03/trumps-populist-mirage/520599/

61. Badiou, A. (2017). *The true life*. Cambridge: Polity, p. 38. Badiou states here, "The second alternative is the reactive desire for a return to traditional – that is, hierarchical – symbolization. The desire is often concealed in the guise of some religious narrative or other, whether it's a question of Protestant sects in the US, reactionary Islam in the Middle East,

or the return to ritualistic Judaism in Europe. But it can also live in nationalistic hierarchies...pure and simple racism."

62. In the same place, p. 37. Badiou states here, "The first is the never-ending defense of capitalism and its empty freedoms," undermined as they are by the sterile neutrality of market determination alone. Let's call this alternative the appeal to what I call "the desire for the West."

63. Brown, W. (2010). *Walled states, waining sovereignty*. New York: Zone Books, p. 24.

64. For a thorough analysis of neoliberalism see, Harvey, D. (2005). *A brief history of neoliberalism*. Oxford: Oxford University Press. Kindle Edition.

65. Badiou, A. (2017). *The true life*. Cambridge: Polity. See chapter 1, "To be young, today: sense and nonsense."

66. Swanson, A. (2017, October 11). Trump's Tough Talk on Nafta Raises Prospects of Pact's Demise. Retrieved October 11, 2017, from https://www.nytimes.com/2017/10/11/business/economy/nafta-trump.html

67. Zizek, S. (n.d.). How to Read Lacan | SLAVOJ ZIZEK. Retrieved January 2, 2018, from http://www.lacan.com/essays/?page_id=261

68. There was, of course, white-collar office work during the period of industrialized capitalism. But this kind of cognitive labor was still run along a "9–5" shift and was markedly different to the cognitive labor that now appears in our postindustrial economy. And, in rural America, there was the reality of local farm communities and agricultural labor.

69. Berardi, F. (2009). *The soul at work: From alienation to autonomy*. Los Angeles, CA: Semiotext(e), pp. 115-117.

70. In the same place.

71. Berry, W. (2010). *What are people for?: essays*. Berkeley, CA: Counterpoint. Kindle Edition, pp. 130-132.

72. In the same place.

73. Brittan, S. (2013, April 18). Thatcher was right - there is

no 'society.' Retrieved October 2, 2017, from https://www.ft.com/content/d1387b70-a5d5-11e2-9b77-00144feabdc0

74. Bateman, O. (2016, October 05). Why the "Safe-Space" Debate Is a Problem for Adjuncts. Retrieved October 5, 2016, from https://www.theatlantic.com/education/archive/2016/10/a-power-struggle-inside-safe-spaces/502859/

75. Buchanan, M. (2002). *Nexus: small worlds and the groundbreaking theory of networks.* New York: W.W. Norton & Company, pp. 41-46.

76. Culkin, B. (2017). *There is no such thing as Boston: gentrification and the disappearance of a city.* Charleston: Create Space. See chapter 3, "Gate of Heaven and the Religion of Yuppies."

77. Vitali, A. (2017, November 27). Trump calls Warren "Pocahontas" at event honoring Native Americans. Retrieved November 27, 2017, from https://www.nbcnews.com/politics/white-house/trump-calls-warren-pocahontas-event-honoring-native-americans-n824266

78. Zizek, S. (2014). *The universal exception.* London: Bloomsbury. p. xv (from Preface to the paperback edition) Zizek states here, in reference to the importance of civility as "the social substance" of autonomous individuals, that "If this substance disintegrates, then the social space of the individual is foreclosed." The point is that, whether it be from overly monitored PC language or Trump's style of brashness, we are in either case witnessing a collapse of our shared social space.

79. Beckwith, R. (2017, October 24). Donald Trump's Twitter Attacks on Bob Corker, Fact Checked. Retrieved October 24, 2017, from http://time.com/4994789/donald-trump-twitter-bob-corker/

80. Berardi, F., Genosko, G., and Thoburn, N. (2011). *After the future.* Edinburgh: AK Press, p. 55.

81. Kevin Kelly (1993). Out of Control: The New Biology of

Machines, Social Systems, and the Economic World, p. 33. Quoted from Berardi, F. (2017). *Futurability: the age of impotence and the horizon of possibility*. Brooklyn: Verso Books. Kindle Edition, Locations 2990-2991.

82. Flood, A. (2017, November 01). Fake news is "very real" word of the year for 2017. Retrieved November 1, 2017, from https://www.theguardian.com/books/2017/nov/02/fake-news-is-very-real-word-of-the-year-for-2017

83. Stolberg, S. G. (2017, October 24). Jeff Flake, a Fierce Trump Critic, Will Not Seek Re-election for Senate. Retrieved October 24, 2017, from https://www.nytimes.com/2017/10/24/us/politics/jeff-flake-arizona.html

Chapter 3

84. Baudrillard, J., Smith, R. G., and Clarke, D. B. (2015). *Jean Baudrillard from hyperreality to disappearance: uncollected interviews*. Edinburgh: Edinburgh University Press. Kindle Edition, Location 3642.

85. Goldman, A., and Rappeport, A. (2016, October 28). Emails in Anthony Weiner Inquiry Jolt Hillary Clinton's Campaign. Retrieved October 31, 2017, from https://www.nytimes.com/2016/10/29/us/politics/fbi-hillary-clinton-email.html

86. Parks, M., Farrington, D., and Taylor, J. (2017, May 15). The James Comey Saga, In Timeline Form. Retrieved December 1, 2017, from https://www.npr.org/2017/05/15/527773206/what-just-happened-the-james-comey-saga-in-timeline-form

87. Holmes, B. (2009). *Escape the overcode: activist art in the control society*. Eindhoven: Van Abbemuseum.

88. Zizek, S. (2012, August 28). Slavoj Zizek: Don't Act. Just Think. Retrieved December 5, 2017, from https://www.youtube.com/watch?v=lgR6uaVqWsQ

89. Zizek, S. (2008). *Violence*. New York: Picador, p. 7.

90. Zizek, S. (2012, August 28). Slavoj Zizek: Don't Act. Just

Think. Retrieved December 5, 2017, from https://www.youtube.com/watch?v=IgR6uaVqWsQ

91. See, Howard, P. K. (2011). *The death of common sense: how law is suffocating America*. New York: Random House, pp. 50-53. Howard states here, "Rationalism, the bright dream of figuring out everything in advance and setting it forth in a centralized regulatory system, has made us blind. Obsessed with certainty, we see almost nothing...Rationalism looms before us with more logic than we can possibly respond to, demanding almost all our energy, but ultimately not making any sense. In other words, *too much* "rationality" — as in trying to portray human life as a mirror of digital, binary logic — forecloses the very possibility of common sense and public space.

92. Trump, D. (2015). *Time to Get Tough: Making America Great Again!* Washington, DC: Regnery Publishing, a division of Salem Media Group, p. 8.

Epilogue

93. Ebert, J. D. (2011). *The new media invasion: digital technologies and the world they unmake*. Jefferson, NC: McFarland & Co., Inc, pp. 23-24.

94. Zizek, S. (2014). *The universal exception*. London: Bloomsbury. See chapter 9, "Multiculturalism, or, the cultural logic of multinational capitalism."

95. Fisher, M. (2010). *Capitalist realism: is there no alternative?* Winchester, UK: Zero Books. Kindle Edition, p. 4.

Bibliography

Andersen, K. (2017). *Fantasyland: how America went haywire: a 500-year history*. New York: Random House.

Aranda, J., and Diederichsen, D. (2011). *Are you working too much?: post-Fordism, precarity, and the labor of art*. Berlin: Sternberg Press. Kindle Edition.

Badiou, A., Gauchet, M., Duru, M., Legros, M., and Spitzer, S. (2016). *What is to be done?: a dialogue on communism, capitalism, and the future of democracy*. Cambridge: Polity. Kindle Edition.

Badiou, A. (2016). *Our wound is not so recent: thinking the Paris killings of 13 November*. Malden, MA: Polity Press. Kindle Edition.

Badiou, A. (2012). *The rebirth of history*. London: Verso.

Badiou, A. (2017). *The true life*. Cambridge: Polity.

Baudrillard, J. (1983). *Simulations*. New York: Semiotext(e).

Baudrillard, J., Smith, R. G., and Clarke, D. B. (2015). *Jean Baudrillard from hyperreality to disappearance: uncollected interviews*. Edinburgh: Edinburgh University Press. Kindle Edition.

Bauman, Z. (2015). *Liquid modernity*. Cambridge, UK: Polity Press.

Berardi, F. (2017). *Futurability: the age of impotence and the horizon of possibility*. Brooklyn: Verso Books. Kindle Edition.

Berardi, F. (2009). *The soul at work*. South Pasadena, CA: Semiotext(e).

Berardi, F., Genosko, G., and Thoburn, N. (2011). *After the future*. Edinburgh: AK Press.

Berry, T., Tucker, M. E., and Grim, J. (2012). *The Christian future and the fate of the earth*. Orbis Books: New York.

Berry, W. (2015). *The unsettling of America: culture & agriculture*. ZULU: Counterpoint. Kindle Edition.

Berry, W. (2010). *What are people for?: essays*. Berkeley, CA: Counterpoint. Kindle Edition.

Berry, W. (2016). *Our only world: ten essays.* Berkeley, CA: Counterpoint. Kindle Edition.

Brown, W. (2010). *Walled states, waining sovereignty.* New York: Zone Books.

Buchanan, M. (2002). *Nexus: small worlds and the groundbreaking theory of networks.* New York: W.W. Norton & Company.

Burchard, B. (2017). *High performance habits: how extraordinary people become that way.* Carlsbad: Hay House, Inc.

Chomsky, N. (2016). *Who rules the world?* New York: Metropolitan Books.

Dionne, E. J., Ornstein, N. J., and Mann, T. E. (2017). *One nation after Trump: a guide for the perplexed, the disillusioned, the desperate, and the not-yet deported.* New York: St. Martins Press.

Ebert, J. D. (2011). *The new media invasion: digital technologies and the world they unmake.* Jefferson, NC: McFarland & Co., Inc.

Fisher, E. (2013). *Media and new capitalism in the digital age: the spirit of networks.* Basingstoke: Palgrave Macmillan.

Fisher, M. (2010). *Capitalist realism: is there no alternative?* Winchester, UK: Zero Books. Kindle Edition.

Frances, A. (2017). *Twilight of American sanity: a psychiatrist analyzes the age of Trump.* New York: HarperCollins.

Friedman, T. L. (2017). *Thank you for being late: an optimist's guide to thriving in the age of accelerations.* New York: Picador.

Galeano, E. (2009). *Open veins of Latin America: five centuries of the pillage of a continent.* London: Profile Books.

Harvey, D. (2005). *A brief history of neoliberalism.* Oxford: Oxford University Press. Kindle Edition.

Holmes, B. (2009). *Escape the overcode: activist art in the control society.* Eindhoven: Van Abbemuseum.

Howard, P. K. (2011). *The death of common sense: how law is suffocating America.* New York: Random House.

Kelly, K. (1993). *Out of control: the new biology of machines, social systems, and the economic world.* New York. Perseus Books.

Kelly, K. (2017) *The inevitable: understanding the 12 technological forces that will shape our future*. New York, NY: Penguin USA.

Lilla, M. (2017). *The once and future liberal: after identity politics.* New York: Harper.

McLuhan, M. (1951). *The mechanical bride: folklore of industrial man.* New York: Vanguard.

Nichols, J. (2017). *Horsemen of the Trumpocalypse: a field guide to the most dangerous people in America.* New York: Nation Books.

Rotella, C. (2004). *Good with their hands: boxers, bluesmen, and other characters from the Rust Belt.* Berkeley, CA: University of California Press.

Srnicek, N. (2017). *Platform capitalism.* Cambridge, UK: Polity. Kindle Edition.

Spence, L. (2015). *Knocking the hustle: against the neoliberal turn in black politics.* Brooklyn, NY: Punctum. Kindle Edition.

Trump, D. (2015). *Time to Get Tough: Making America Great Again!* Washington, DC: Regnery Publishing, a division of Salem Media Group.

Williams, A., and Snricek, N. (2015). *Inventing the future: postcapitalism and a world without work.* Brooklyn: Verso.

Zizek, S. (2016). *Against the double blackmail: refugees, terror and other troubles with the neighbours.* London: Penguin Books.

Zizek, S. (2008). *For they know not what they do: enjoyment as a political factor.* London: Verso.

Zizek, S. (2014). *The universal exception.* London: Bloomsbury.

Zizek, S. (2014). *Event: a philosophical journey through a concept.* London: Melville House.

Zizek, S. (2008). *Violence.* New York: Picador.

Zero Books

CULTURE, SOCIETY & POLITICS

Contemporary culture has eliminated the concept and public figure of the intellectual. A cretinous anti-intellectualism presides, cheer-led by hacks in the pay of multinational corporations who reassure their bored readers that there is no need to rouse themselves from their stupor. Zer0 Books knows that another kind of discourse – intellectual without being academic, popular without being populist – is not only possible: it is already flourishing. Zer0 is convinced that in the unthinking, blandly consensual culture in which we live, critical and engaged theoretical reflection is more important than ever before.

If you have enjoyed this book, why not tell other readers by posting a review on your preferred book site.

Recent bestsellers from Zero Books are:

In the Dust of This Planet
Horror of Philosophy vol. 1
Eugene Thacker
In the first of a series of three books on the Horror of
Philosophy, *In the Dust of This Planet* offers the genre of horror
as a way of thinking about the unthinkable.
Paperback: 978-1-84694-676-9 ebook: 978-1-78099-010-1

Capitalist Realism
Is there no alternative?
Mark Fisher
An analysis of the ways in which capitalism has presented itself
as the only realistic political-economic system.
Paperback: 978-1-84694-317-1 ebook: 978-1-78099-734-6

Rebel Rebel
Chris O'Leary
David Bowie: every single song. Everything you want to know,
everything you didn't know.
Paperback: 978-1-78099-244-0 ebook: 978-1-78099-713-1

Cartographies of the Absolute
Alberto Toscano, Jeff Kinkle
An aesthetics of the economy for the twenty-first century.
Paperback: 978-1-78099-275-4 ebook: 978-1-78279-973-3

Malign Velocities
Accelerationism and Capitalism
Benjamin Noys
Long listed for the Bread and Roses Prize 2015, *Malign Velocities* argues against the need for speed, tracking acceleration as the symptom of the ongoing crises of capitalism.
Paperback: 978-1-78279-300-7 ebook: 978-1-78279-299-4

Meat Market
Female Flesh under Capitalism
Laurie Penny
A feminist dissection of women's bodies as the fleshy fulcrum of capitalist cannibalism, whereby women are both consumers and consumed.
Paperback: 978-1-84694-521-2 ebook: 978-1-84694-782-7

Poor but Sexy
Culture Clashes in Europe East and West
Agata Pyzik
How the East stayed East and the West stayed West.
Paperback: 978-1-78099-394-2 ebook: 978-1-78099-395-9

Romeo and Juliet in Palestine
Teaching Under Occupation
Tom Sperlinger
Life in the West Bank, the nature of pedagogy and the role of a university under occupation.
Paperback: 978-1-78279-637-4 ebook: 978-1-78279-636-7

Readers of ebooks can buy or view any of these bestsellers by clicking on the live link in the title. Most titles are published in paperback and as an ebook. Paperbacks are available in traditional bookshops. Both print and ebook formats are available online.

Find more titles and sign up to our readers' newsletter at http://www.johnhuntpublishing.com/culture-and-politics

Follow us on Facebook
at https://www.facebook.com/ZeroBooks

and Twitter at https://twitter.com/Zer0Books